First World War
and Army of Occupation
War Diary
France, Belgium and Germany

1 INDIAN CAVALRY DIVISION
Lucknow Cavalry Brigade
36 Jacobs Horse
31 August 1914 - 31 December 1916

WO95/1174/4

The Naval & Military Press Ltd
www.nmarchive.com
Published in association with The National Archives

Published by

The Naval & Military Press Ltd

Unit 10 Ridgewood Industrial Park,

Uckfield, East Sussex,

TN22 5QE England

Tel: +44 (0) 1825 749494

www.naval-military-press.com

www.nmarchive.com

This diary has been reprinted in facsimile from the original. Any imperfections are inevitably reproduced and the quality may fall short of modern type and cartographic standards.

© Crown Copyright
Images reproduced by permission of The National Archives, London, England, 2015.

Contents

Document type	Place/Title	Date From	Date To
Heading	WO95/1174/4		
Heading	B.E.F. 1 Ind. Cav. Div. Lucknow Bde 36 Jacobs Horse. 1914 Aug to 1916 Dec		
Heading	War Diary of the 36th Jacob's Horse. From 31st August 1914 To 2nd January 1915		
War Diary	Cawnpore	31/08/1914	10/10/1914
War Diary	Bombay	12/10/1914	16/10/1914
War Diary	Harseilles	08/11/1914	11/11/1914
War Diary	Orleans	13/11/1914	08/12/1914
War Diary	Lillers	10/12/1914	10/12/1914
War Diary	Rombly	22/12/1914	22/12/1914
War Diary	Ham En Artois	23/12/1914	25/12/1914
War Diary	Predefin-Ranneville-Palfart	25/12/1914	30/12/1914
War Diary	Predefin-Ranneville-Palfart-Livossart	31/12/1914	02/01/1915
Heading	War Diary of 36th Jacobs Horse. From 1st January 1915 To 31st January 1915		
War Diary	Predefin-Ranneville-Palfart-Livossart	03/01/1915	08/01/1915
War Diary	Festubert	09/01/1915	11/01/1915
War Diary	Bethune	12/01/1915	12/01/1915
War Diary	Predefin	12/01/1915	12/01/1915
War Diary	Festubert	09/01/1915	11/01/1915
War Diary	Predefin	13/01/1915	31/01/1915
War Diary	321-Sabro	09/01/1915	10/01/1915
War Diary	Festubert	10/01/1915	12/01/1915
Heading	War Diary of 36th Jacobs Horse From 1st February 1915 To 28th February 1915		
War Diary	Predefin Palfart & Livossart	01/02/1915	28/02/1915
Heading	War Diary of 36th Jacobs Horse. From 1st March 1915 To 31st March 1915		
War Diary	Predefin Palfart & Livossart	01/03/1915	07/03/1915
War Diary	Palfart & Livossart	08/03/1915	12/03/1915
War Diary	Auchel	13/03/1915	14/03/1915
War Diary	Febvin	15/03/1915	18/03/1915
War Diary	Liettres & Linghem	19/03/1915	31/03/1915
Heading	War Diary of 36th Jacobs Horse From 1st April 1915 To 30th April 1915		
War Diary	Liettres & Linghem	01/04/1915	24/04/1915
War Diary	Oxelaere	25/04/1915	28/04/1915
War Diary	St. Jean-Ter-Biezen	29/04/1915	30/04/1915
Heading	War Diary of 36th Jacob's Horse From 1st May 1915 To 31st May 1915		
War Diary	St Jean-Ter-Biezen	01/05/1915	01/05/1915
War Diary	Oxelaere	02/05/1915	04/05/1915
War Diary	Marthes-Ham-Blessy	05/05/1915	17/05/1915
War Diary	Reveillon	18/05/1915	18/05/1915
War Diary	Burbure	18/05/1915	19/05/1915
War Diary	Marthes Ham & Blessy	20/05/1915	27/05/1915
War Diary	Oxelaere	27/05/1915	28/05/1915
War Diary	L'Erklesbrugge	28/05/1915	28/05/1915
War Diary	Brandhoek	29/05/1915	31/05/1915

Heading	War Diary of 36th Jacobs Horse From 1st June 1915 To 30th June 1915		
War Diary	Brandhoek L'Erklesbrugge	01/06/1915	01/06/1915
War Diary	Brandhoek	02/06/1915	03/06/1915
War Diary	Yeoman's Post	03/06/1915	04/06/1915
War Diary	G.H.Q. Line	04/06/1915	04/06/1915
War Diary	Yeoman's Post	05/06/1915	05/06/1915
War Diary	Brandhoek L'Erklesbrugge	06/06/1915	11/06/1915
War Diary	Brandhoek	12/06/1915	15/06/1915
War Diary	Blessy & Ham	16/06/1915	16/06/1915
War Diary	Marthes Ham & Blessy	17/06/1915	30/06/1915
Heading	War Diary of 36th Jacob's Horse. From 1st July 1915 To 31st July 1915		
War Diary	Marthes Ham & Blessy	01/07/1915	31/07/1915
War Diary	War Diary of 36th Jacob's Horse From 1st August 1915 To 31st August 1915		
War Diary	Fruges	01/08/1915	01/08/1915
War Diary	Ecquemicourt	02/08/1915	02/08/1915
War Diary	Ribeaucourt	03/08/1915	03/08/1915
War Diary	Berteaucourt Les Dames	04/08/1915	08/08/1915
War Diary	Halloys	08/08/1915	13/08/1915
War Diary	Berteaucourt-Les-Dames	14/08/1915	22/08/1915
War Diary	Forceville Bivouac	23/08/1915	23/08/1915
War Diary	Authvile	24/08/1915	24/08/1915
War Diary	Berteaucourt Les Dames	24/08/1915	24/08/1915
War Diary	Authvile	25/08/1915	25/08/1915
War Diary	Berteaucourt Les Dames	25/08/1915	31/08/1915
Heading	War Diary of 36th Jacob's Horse from 1st September 1915 To 30th September 1915		
War Diary	Authvile	26/08/1915	02/09/1915
War Diary	Berteaucourt-Les-Dames	02/09/1915	12/09/1915
War Diary	Authvile	13/09/1915	17/09/1915
War Diary	Berteaucourt Les Dames	18/09/1915	22/09/1915
War Diary	Longuevillette	22/09/1915	30/09/1915
Heading	War Diary of 36th Jacob's Horse. From 1st October 1915 To 31st October 1915		
War Diary	Longuevillette	01/10/1915	13/10/1915
War Diary	Bernaville	14/10/1915	21/10/1915
War Diary	Oissy Riencourt & Lemesge	22/10/1915	31/10/1915
Heading	War Diary of 36th Jacob's Horse From 1st November 1915 To 30th November 1915		
War Diary	Oissy, Riencourt & Lemesge	01/11/1915	17/11/1915
War Diary	Fontaine, Wanel & Sorel	18/11/1915	30/11/1915
War Diary	Oissy, Riencourt & Lemesge	01/11/1915	17/11/1915
War Diary	Fontaine, Wanel & Sorel	18/11/1915	30/11/1915
Heading	The D.A.G., G.H.Q. 3rd Echelon A.G. in India	27/12/1915	27/12/1915
War Diary	Oissy, Riencourt & Lemesge	01/11/1915	17/11/1915
War Diary	Fontaine Wanel & Sorel	18/11/1915	30/11/1915
Heading	War Diary of 36th Jacob's Horse From 1st December 1915 To 31st December 1915		
War Diary	Fontaine, Sorel & Wanel	01/12/1915	15/12/1915
War Diary	Franleu Campagne Hymmeville Frireulles	16/12/1915	31/12/1915
Heading	War Diary of 36th Jacob's Horse From 1st January 1916 To 31st January 1916		
War Diary	Franleu Campagne Hymmeville Frireulles	01/01/1916	31/01/1916

Heading	War Diary of 36th Jacob's Horse From 1st February 1916 To 29th February 1916		
War Diary	Franleu Campagne Hymmeville Frireulles	01/02/1916	29/02/1916
Heading	War Diary of 36th Jacob's Horse From 1st March 1916 To 31st March 1916		
War Diary	Franleu Campagne Hymmeville Frireulles	01/03/1916	25/03/1916
War Diary	Boufflers and Genne-Ivergny Via Canchy and Le Boisle	26/03/1916	31/03/1916
Heading	War Diary of 36th Jacob's Horse From 1st April 1916 To 30th April 1916		
War Diary	Boufflers and Genne-Ivergny	01/04/1916	08/04/1916
War Diary	Gapennes	09/04/1916	15/04/1916
War Diary	Boufflers & Genne-Ivergny	15/04/1916	30/04/1916
War Diary	War Diary of 36th Jacob's Horse From 1st May 1916 To 31st May 1916		
War Diary	Boufflers Genne-Ivergny	01/05/1916	01/05/1916
War Diary	St Riquier	01/05/1916	07/05/1916
War Diary	Boufflers Genne-Ivergny	07/05/1916	09/05/1916
War Diary	Moncheaux	10/05/1916	31/05/1916
Heading	War Diary of 36th Jacob's Horse. From 1st June 1916 To 30th June 1916		
War Diary	Moncheaux	01/06/1916	21/06/1916
War Diary	Neuville St Vaast	21/06/1916	27/06/1916
War Diary	Moncheaux	28/06/1916	29/06/1916
War Diary	Bout Des Pres	30/06/1916	30/06/1916
War Diary	War Diary of 36th Jacob's Horse From 1st July 1916 To 31st July 1916		
War Diary	Bout Des Pres	01/07/1916	02/07/1916
War Diary	Villers L'Hopital	03/07/1916	18/07/1916
War Diary	Villers Brulin	19/07/1916	30/07/1916
Heading	War Diary of 36th Jacob's Horse From 1st August 1916 To 31st August 1916		
War Diary	Villers Brulin	01/08/1916	09/08/1916
War Diary	Gaudiempre	09/08/1916	15/08/1916
War Diary	Coullemont	21/08/1916	29/08/1916
War Diary	War Diary of 36th Jacob's Horse From 1st September 1916 To 30th September 1916		
War Diary	Coullemont	01/09/1916	02/09/1916
War Diary	Remaisnil	03/09/1916	03/09/1916
War Diary	Gapennes	04/09/1916	04/09/1916
War Diary	Beauvoir Riviere	11/09/1916	11/09/1916
War Diary	Hem	12/09/1916	12/09/1916
War Diary	Qverrier	13/09/1916	13/09/1916
War Diary	Querrieu	14/09/1916	14/09/1916
War Diary	Ville-Sous-Corbie Dernancourt	15/09/1916	23/09/1916
War Diary	Dernancourt	24/09/1916	25/09/1916
War Diary	Mametz	26/09/1916	27/09/1916
War Diary	Dernancourt Bussy	27/09/1916	27/09/1916
War Diary	Crouy	28/09/1916	28/09/1916
War Diary	Pont Remy	29/09/1916	29/09/1916
War Diary	Crecy	30/09/1916	30/09/1916
Heading	War Diary of 36th Jacob's Horse From 1st October 1916 To 30th November 1916		
War Diary	Crecy	01/10/1916	01/11/1916
War Diary	Quesnoy Le Montant	02/11/1916	27/11/1916

Heading	War Diary of 36th Jacob's Horse (I.A) From 1st December 1916 To 31st December 1916		
War Diary	Quesnoy Le Montant	01/12/1916	31/12/1916

WO 95/11744/4

B.E.F

1 Ind. Cav. Div.

Lucknow Bde.

36 Jacobs Horse.

1914 Aug to 1916 Dec

WAR DIARY

OF THE

36TH JACOB'S HORSE.

From 31st August 1914 To 2nd January 1915.

P.I.

Army Form C. 2118.

WAR DIARY
or
INTELLIGENCE SUMMARY.

(Erase heading not required.)

Instructions regarding War Diaries and Intelligence Summaries are contained in F. S. Regs., Part II, and the Staff Manual respectively. Title pages will be prepared in manuscript.

[Stamp: ADJUTANT GENERAL INDIA BASE OFFICE 22. JAN. 1915]

[Stamp: No 3 Section A.G's Office at Base I.E. Force Passed to ___ S. Sec[n] on ___]

of Jodhpur Horse

Hour, Date, Place.		Summary of Events and Information.	Remarks and references to Appendices
Midnight 31/8/14 - 1/9/14.	CAWNPORE	Order to Mobilize received. Reservists recalled.	
30/9/14.	CAWNPORE	Mobilization completed.	
6 pm. 8/x/14.	CAWNPORE	Hd Qrs Hd. the entrained & left for Bombay. Arrived 10/x/14. 6 pm.	
6 am. 9/x/14.	CAWNPORE	1½ Sqdn entrained & left for Bombay. Arrived 11/x/14. 6 pm	
9. am. 10/x/14.	CAWNPORE	1½ Sqdn entrained & left for Bombay. Arrived 12/x/14. 9 am.	
12/x/14.	BOMBAY	Hd. Qr. Hd. Qrs. and 2 Sqdn (A & D) embarked on S.S. LAOMEDON at VICTORIA DOCK. Ships left harbour and lay out in the stream. Heat very great.	
15/x/14.	BOMBAY	2 Sqdns (B&C) embarked on S.S. PANDIT.	
16/x/14.		Convoy 45 ships left BOMBAY at 5 pm. S.S. LAOMEDON following S.S. BALLARAT & followed by S.S. PANDIT.	

P.II.

Army Form O. 2118.

WAR DIARY
or
INTELLIGENCE SUMMARY.
(Erase heading not required.)

Instructions regarding War Diaries and Intelligence Summaries are contained in F. S. Regs., Part II, and the Staff Manual respectively. Title pages will be prepared in manuscript.

Hour, Date, Place.	Summary of Events and Information.	Remarks and references to Appendices
MARSEILLES. 9th 19th hour.	Disembarked. Drew new rifle ammunition. Went into camp on Race Course.	R&R
do. 11h hour.	Entrained in 3 trains. Proceeded to ORLEANS.	R&R
ORLEANS. 13th 14th hour.	Detrained. Went into camp at LA SOURCE. Took over new M.G. Weather very wet at first + then cold & frosty.	R&R
do. 8' do.	Entrained in 4 trains. Proceeded to LILLERS.	R&R
LILLERS. 10' do.	Arrived LILLERS. Went into billets	R&R
ROMBLY 22 Dec.	Moved into billets at ROMBLY. ARTOIS. Heavy rain.	R&R
HAM EN ARTOIS. Dec 23.	Moved into billets. 6 A.T. carts & drivers added to Transport Establishment for the carriage of horse rugs.	R&R
" Dec. 24	Lieut. C. F. Orthwaz rejoined from 3rd Hussars.	R&R
" Dec 25	Moved into new billets at PREDEFIN - As follows:- A + B + D Sqdns at PREDEFIN C " at RANNEVILLE and PALFART.	R&R
PREDEFIN - RANNEVILLE - PALFART	Horses much worse but well in short	R&R

Gulab Singh & Sons, Calcutta—No. 22 Army C.—5-8-14—1,07,000.

P.3

Army Form C. 2118.

1914 - 1915

WAR DIARY

or

INTELLIGENCE SUMMARY.

(Erase heading not required.)

Instructions regarding War Diaries and Intelligence Summaries are contained in F. S. Regs., Part II, and the Staff Manual respectively. Title pages will be prepared in manuscript.

Hour, Date, Place.	Summary of Events and Information.	Remarks and references to Appendices
December 28th/1914. PREDEFIN - RANNEVILLE - PALFART. & DL	Orders received to be ready to march into new billets at BOYAVAL and EPS (two miles).	RR
Dec. 29th " "	Orders cancelled & Regt. into new billets. Billetting party returned.	RR
Dec. 30th " "	Owing to shortage of water "D" Sqdn. moved into new billets at LIVOSSART	RR
PREDEFIN - RANNEVILLE - PALFART - LIVOSSART. Dec. 31st	Billets. 1 am. Cr. Attrd Samual returned from Amn. Column. 7 am. Cr. Van Muhenen attached to Amn. Column.	RR
	1915	
Jan. 1. " " "	Billets.	RR
Jan. 2. " " "	Orders received to have 3 nos. Machine gun teams.	RR

WAR DIARY

of 36. Jacobs Horse.

From 1st January 1915. To 31st January 1915.

P.4
Army Form C. 2118.

WAR DIARY of the 36th JACOB'S HORSE
or
INTELLIGENCE SUMMARY

1915

(Erase heading not required.)

PREDEFIN – RANNEVILLE BILUL – PALFART – LIVOSSART.

Hour, Date, Place.	Summary of Events and Information.	Remarks and references to Appendices
Jan. 3rd		
Jan 4th " "	Lt. Col. N.S. Rowe proceeded on 4 days leave to England.	RR
	Major C.H. Alexander transferred to Hospital sick.	
	(Capt. A.U. Gavin Jones & Capt. W.T. Allen 23rd Cavalry (attd. to Reg't) with Jem. Sundara Singh 2 Sowars and 81 horses joined from Base.	
	48 horses	
	Orders received that the Lucknow Cav. Bde. is to destroy in the trenches from evening 9 Thos.	RR
Jan 5th " "	Regiment took part in Brigade Route March Instruction in Point throwing	RR
	10 horses received from 2 g.F. Lancers	
Jan 6th " " "	Butteb – Bomb throwing instruction	RR

P. 5.

Army Form C. 2118.

1915

WAR DIARY of the 36th JACOB'S HORSE.

or

INTELLIGENCE SUMMARY.

(Erase heading not required.)

Instructions regarding War Diaries and Intelligence Summaries are contained in F. S. Regs., Part II, and the Staff Manual respectively. Title pages will be prepared in manuscript.

Hour, Date, Place.	Summary of Events and Information.	Remarks and references to Appendices
Jan 7th PREDEFIN. RANNEVILLE. PALFART LIVOSSART.	Billets - Instruction in Bom[b] throwing - Below research & detachment for trenches	Appendix A.
Jan 8th " "	2nd/Lt R.S. Borne rejoined from leave. Transport & trench party dispatched to BETHUNE	ReR
Jan 9th " " FESTUBERT	The Regt: Strength 11 BOs 141 o.s. Rank & file Entrained at 12.15 P.M. reached BETHUNE at 5 P.M. marched on foot to FESTUBERT & relieved the 19th Lancers in the trenches at 8 P.M. The remainder of the Regt was left in their billets with the horses.	Appx A. Appx A. ReR
Jan 10th FESTUBERT	In the trenches - Capt F. DAVIDSON rejoined at FESTUBERT from leave. A & C Sqns relieved in the firing line trenches at 6 P.M. by B & D Sqns	Appx. A.
Jan 11th FESTUBERT	During the night orders were received to evacuate firing line trenches on account of them being flooded & to take up the support trenches as the firing line This was done before dawn. 2 Corps S.W. Boundero were held as a local reserve & arrived before daylight. The Regiment was relieved in the trenches by the 38th C. I. H and	ReR

Gulab Singh & Sons, Calcutta.—No. 22 Army C.—5-8-14—1,07,000.

P.6
Army Form C. 2118.

WAR DIARY of the 36th JACOB'S HORSE.

or

INTELLIGENCE SUMMARY.

(Erase heading not required.)

Instructions regarding War Diaries and Intelligence
Summaries are contained in F. S. Regs., Part II,
and the Staff Manual respectively. Title pages
will be prepared in manuscript.

Hour, Date, Place.	Summary of Events and Information.	Remarks and references to Appendices
1.20 A.M. Jan. 12. BETHUNE	Marched to BETHUNE on foot starting at 8.12 P.M. reaching there about 10.30 P.M. Regiment entrained and reached their old fields at 8.30 A.M.	
8.30 A.M. " " FREDERIN	A cold frosty night changing to rain in the morning. Officers present at FESTUBERT.	
	B. O. S	
	Lt. Col. R.S. ROOME. Com and	
	Capt. H. ALLARDICE - Adjt.	
	Lieut. M. E. PARNELL. Offr. in Command of Machine Guns.	
	Capt. A. CAMPBELL MUNRO I.M.S. Medical Officer.	
	Major E. A. FAGAN. "C" Sqn.	
	Major W. H. GREEN "A" "	
	Capt. H. M. DAVIDSON D "	
	" A. N. GAVIN-JONES D "	
	" M M CARPENDALE B "	
	Lieut. R. OWEN JONES C Sqn	
	Capt. W. T. ALLEN (23rd Cav.d) A Sqn	
	Interpreter.	
	On: WOODCOCK	
	Mons. BERGASSE.	

P.7.

Army Form C. 2118.

1915.
WAR DIARY of the 36th JACOB'S HORSE.
or
INTELLIGENCE SUMMARY.

(Erase heading not required.)

Instructions regarding War Diaries and Intelligence Summaries are contained in F. S. Regs., Part II, and the Staff Manual respectively. Title pages will be prepared in manuscript.

Hour, Date, Place.	Summary of Events and Information.	Remarks and references to Appendices
Jan 9th, 10th, 11th. FESTUBERT.	Casualties at FESTUBERT. Lieut R. OWEN-JONES - wounded right arm. A NATIVE RANKS. Killed Jemadar SHAM SINGH.. "A" Sqdn No 2652.. Infdr.. UMEDALI SHAH.. "C" Sqdn No 2149.. L/Dafdr.. BAKHTAWAR SINGH. "A" Sqdn No 2773.. Sowr.. SAUTA SINGH ... "A" Sq No 2978 " .... NUR KHAN ... "C" No 3032.. L/Dafdr.. ABDUL AZIZ KHAN. "C" No 3091.. Sowr ... FATEH MOHAMED.D Total 7 killed Wounded No 3006.. Sowr.. DUMMAN SINGH ... A Sqdn No 2880.. " .. AYAN SINGH ... " No 2426.. " .. UTTAM SINGH .... " No 2870.. " .. GULMAHAMED KHAN ... C " No 3020.. " .. BAHADUR KHAN ... C .	RAR

P. 8.
Army Form C. 2118.

1915

WAR DIARY of the 36th JACOB'S HORSE.
or
INTELLIGENCE SUMMARY.

(Erase heading not required.)

Instructions regarding War Diaries and Intelligence Summaries are contained in F. S. Regs., Part II, and the Staff Manual respectively. Title pages will be prepared in manuscript.

Hour, Date, Place.	Summary of Events and Information.	Remarks and references to Appendices
Jan. 9th, 10th – 11th FESTUBERT (contd)	Wounded Con<u>td</u> No 2047 ..... L<u>ce</u> D<u>ffr</u>. MOHAMED KHAN ..... Sq<u>dn</u> No 22 ..... Sow<u>t</u> MARIAM SINGH ..... A " No 61 ..... " BAGUL ..... C " No 2607 ..... L<u>ce</u> D<u>ffr</u> DASUNDA SINGH ..... A " No 1906 ..... Sow<u>t</u> BHAN SINGH ..... A No 3048 ..... " AMIR SHAH ..... B No 2996 ..... " JALLAL SHAH ..... B Total 12 Total. 13.O. wounded. 1.I.O. Killed 6 Rank & file Killed 12 ..... wounded. Casualties 20.	RR

P.9.
Army Form C. 2118.

1915

WAR DIARY of the 36th JACOB'S HORSE.

or

INTELLIGENCE SUMMARY.

(Erase heading not required.)

Instructions regarding War Diaries and Intelligence Summaries are contained in F. S. Regs., Part II, and the Staff Manual respectively. Title pages will be prepared in manuscript.

Hour, Date, Place.	Summary of Events and Information.	Remarks and references to Appendices
Jan 13th. PREDEFIN.	Approximately 225 men were affected in their feet by the immersion in the cold water of the trenches. Most of them getting rapidly better. Men cheerful. Major E.A. FAGAN Capt. M.M. CARPENDALE } granted 5 days leave to ENGLAND. Weather - rainy but mild.	Copy Divisional Letters of 16.1.1915. G.O.C. 1st I.C. Div. wishes to express his appreciation of the gallant conduct of the United Ptn Indian Officers & men noted below on January 10th Capt. E.A.M.ARDICE 36th J.H. escorted men who were wounded when under heavy fire. [signed] RuR
Jan 14th "	Lieut. M.E. PARNELL granted 5 days leave to ENGLAND. [signed] RuR Weather - rainy but mild.	RuR
Jan 15th "	Lieut. M.E. PARNELL granted 5 days leave to ENGLAND. Weather - rainy but mild.	RuR
Jan 16th "	Weather rainy but mild. Regiment took part in a divisional Parade.	RuR

P. 10.

Army Form C. 2118.

1915.

WAR DIARY of the 36th JACOB'S HORSE

or

INTELLIGENCE SUMMARY.

(Erase heading not required.)

Instructions regarding War Diaries and Intelligence Summaries are contained in F. S. Regs., Part II, and the Staff Manual respectively. Title pages will be prepared in manuscript.

Hour, Date, Place.	Summary of Events and Information.	Remarks and references to Appendices
Jan. 17th PREDEFIN.	Billets. Lieut. E.G. ATKINSON. 17th Cav. (attd.) having been transferred to the Signal Squadron to which off the strength of the Regiment. Rainy but mild.	PPR
Jan. 18th "	The Regt. took part, with the Brigade, in a Scheme covering the Concentration of the Cavalry Corps. Snowed last night & during the day till noon when it thawed slightly.	PPR
Jan. 19th " "	Billets. Thawing slightly - fine.	PPR
Jan. 20th " "	Billets - rain	PPR
Jan. 21st " "	Billets - rain	PPR

P11
1915
WAR DIARY of the 36th JACOBS HORSE.
or
INTELLIGENCE SUMMARY.
Army Form C. 2118.

(Erase heading not required.)

Hour, Date, Place.	Summary of Events and Information.	Remarks and references to Appendices
Jan 22. PREDEFIN.	Divisional Reserve – Fine, slight frost in morning. RR	
Jan 23rd "	Capt A. Marshall 28th (Can) joined – Jem. SANT SINGH & 6 men 23rd (Car) joined as 2nd in command. RR Rain.	
Jan 24th "	Billets – Rain & mud RR	
Jan 25th "	Brigade Reserve. Mud. "Crab wamu" mounted lorries" moved to Regiment. RR	
Jan 26th "	Billets – Snow. Capes travelled" moved to Regiment. Cross Roads discontinued. RR	
Jan 27th "	Brigade on duty from 8 am today till 8 am 28th mg. RR	
Jan 28th "	Billets. Hard frost. RR	

P.12

Army Form C. 2118.

1915.
WAR DIARY of the 36th Jacob's Horse.
or
INTELLIGENCE SUMMARY.
(Erase heading not required.)

Instructions regarding War Diaries and Intelligence Summaries are contained in F. S. Regs., Part II, and the Staff Manual respectively. Title pages will be prepared in manuscript.

Hour, Date, Place.		Summary of Events and Information.	Remarks and references to Appendices
Jan 29th PREDEFIN.		Regiment took part in a Divisional Surprise.	
		Capt. D.S. STEWART 17th "Car." Joined.	
	11.35 P.M.	Regiment warned to hold itself in readiness. 36 J.H. joined as reinforcement	R.R.
		Fine day.	
Jan 30th — do —		Regiment still in readiness.	
		Fine day. Cold.	R.R.
Jan 31st do		Lieut. the Honble A.R. ADDINGTON 27th L"Car" joined.	
		Snowed all day.	R.R.
		Regiment still in readiness.	
	176. Mesopotamia.	Extract from Brigade Orders of 15.1.15.	
		The Brigadier General Commanding wishes to place on record his appreciation and thanks for the fine spirit of endurance and cheerfulness in abnormal conditions shown by all ranks of the Brigade during the operations 9th to 10th January.	
		(True Extract) T.B.Romwell Lt. Col.	

P 13

Army Form C. 2118.

1915
WAR DIARY of the 36th Jacob's Horse.
or
INTELLIGENCE SUMMARY.

(Erase heading not required.)

Instructions regarding War Diaries and Intelligence Summaries are contained in F. S. Regs., Part II, and the Staff Manual respectively. Title pages will be prepared in manuscript.

Hour, Date, Place.	Summary of Events and Information.	Remarks and references to Appendices
PREDEFIN Jan. 31.	List of British Officers present during the month. Lt. Col. R.E. RODWE. Comd. Major C.H. ALEXANDER. admitted Hospital 4th Inst. Major S.A. FAGAN. " W.G. GREEN. Capt. H.M. DAVIDSON. " A.N. GAVIN-JONES. " M.M. CARPENDALE. " H.B. ALLARDICE. Adjut. Lieut C.F. CAHUSAC. " M.E. PARNELL. Q.M. " R.D. OWEN-JONES. wounded 10.75. admitted into Hospital 10.5. Capt. A.C. MUNRO. IMS. Med. Officer. <u>Attached Officers</u> Capt. W. TALLEN. 23rd Cav. admitted Hospital 14th Inst. Capt. A. MARSHALL 28th L/Cav. Joined 2.3.75. " H.S. STEWART. 17th Cav. " 29.75. Lt. F.G. ATKINSON 17th Cav. Transfd to Div. Signal Cy. and 1st M.C.D. 16.75. Lt. R.A. ADDINGTON. 26th Cav. Joined 31.75. RER	

Gulab Singh & Sons, Calcutta—No. 22 Army C—7-5-14—1,07,000.

P.I

1915"

WAR DIARY of the 36th JACOB'S HORSE.
or
INTELLIGENCE SUMMARY.

Army Form C. 2118.

(Erase heading not required.)

No 3 Section Appendix A.
A. G's Office at Base
I. E. Force
Passed to .... S. Sect.
on 7 - 2 - 15

Hour, Date, Place.	Summary of Events and Information.	Remarks and references to Appendices
Jan 9th		
11. 13.05	The Reg't strength as per margin paraded at 11AM at their billets on foot. At 12.15 PM (the train being 1½ hours late) the Reg't entrained in 13 trucks & reached BETHUNE 5 PM.	
14. 1.05	Detrained and marched on foot to FESTUBERT and relieved the 19th Lancers in the trenches. — The relief was complete by 10 P.M. The Brigade was distributed in the trenches as under.	
321. Sabres	Right section. Jamming up with Black Watch alignment - 36 Jacob's Horse	
	Centre section. 29th Deccan Horse.	
	Left section. 1st K.E. Grants.	
	The Reg't was disposed of as follows: — A & C Sqdn firing line	
	B Sqdn support. D Sqdn Reserve.	
	The enemy had called for to Korea heepolacke which lit up the country and A & C Squadrons fired on heavily. & going up the road to the trenches. — The communicating trenches were so full of water, that they could not be used.	
	No real casualties took place on this relief.	

P 2

1915

Army Form C. 2118.

Appendix A.

WAR DIARY
or
INTELLIGENCE SUMMARY.
(Erase heading not required.)

Instructions regarding War Diaries and Intelligence Summaries are contained in F. S. Regs., Part II, and the Staff Manual respectively. Title pages will be prepared in manuscript.

Hour, Date, Place.	Summary of Events and Information.	Remarks and references to Appendices
Jan. 9.	The trenches were full of water. We were being up to their knees and the water was rising. Beyond steadily firing at night no incidents. The night was cold & there was no wind.	
Jan. 10. 8 A.M.	Cap H. M. DAVIDSON returned from short leave at FESTUBERT	
3.45 A.M.	Beginning after heavy — In order to prepare for and co-operate in an attack by No 2 wd Infantry Bde South of Canal the G.O.C. 1st Bt. Bde ordered following to be carried out to day AAA 10.55 A.M burst of rifle fire on German trenches in our front AAA 1.45 till 1.50 P.M burst of rifle fire AAA 1.50 till 2 P.M ordering chiefs all trenches for 10 minutes AAA 3 P.M. attack by infantry during and after this attack we are to keep up steady fire to prevent Germans from reinforcing the attacked point. The above orders were carried out. After the bombardment at 3 P.M. the Germans	

P. 3

Army Form C. 2118.

Appendix A

1915.

WAR DIARY
or
INTELLIGENCE SUMMARY.

(Erase heading not required.)

Instructions regarding War Diaries and Intelligence Summaries are contained in F. S. Regs., Part II, and the Staff Manual respectively. Title pages will be prepared in manuscript.

Hour, Date, Place.	Summary of Events and Information.	Remarks and references to Appendices
Jan. 10th FESTUBERT	Artillery replied. The only casualties they met was to free house at Southern end of village. The shells fell all round the village.	
3.30 PM	Lt. R. D. BAILEY - TOMES wounded in the trenches.	
5 – 6 PM	A & C Sqdns relieved in the trenches by B & D Sqdns. A Sqdn not relieved. Support and "C" Sqdn in reserve. All ranks very done by their long time service in the trenches. Many men suffering from frostbite & swollen legs feet. Hot tea & hot rum & water had been prepared for them also dry socks. In the morro of the deserted village, the latter was a mistake. The men should have been made to wash their feet in cold water, eaten hot khana, grove near a fire, circulation should have been restored by friction. Change of socks should have been taken.	

Gulab Singh & Sons, Calcutta—No. 22 Army C.—5-8-14—1,07,000.

P.4
Army Form C. 2118.

Appendix A

1915
WAR DIARY
or
INTELLIGENCE SUMMARY.
(Erase heading not required.)

Instructions regarding War Diaries and Intelligence Summaries are contained in F. S. Regs., Part II, and the Staff Manual respectively. Title pages will be prepared in manuscript.

Hour, Date, Place.	Summary of Events and Information.	Remarks and references to Appendices
Jan. 10th FESTUBERT	During the night orders were received to vacate the front line Trenches & move back to the support trenches, moving to the front line Trenches being untenable, the Trenches having more then filled with.	
Jan 11th 4 – 6 A.M.	The 2 detached Coys (B&D) were withdrawn without incident and the following line taken up:— Firing line B & D Coys in former support Trenches N.E. side of village. — D Coy Continued line to road leading between E & P y le PLANTIN. Support A & C Coys in village. – Local reserve one double Coy South West Borderers (which had arrived at 5 A.M.) in entrenchments between F. P. y le PLANTIN.	
1.55 P.M.	A kind of fire on Enemys Trenches also bombardment by Artillery	
2 P.M.	Enemy replied by shelling village, support Trenches & Ground in vicinity and nearby roads.	
6 – 8 P.M.	Regiment relieved by 38th Central India Horse.	

P 5-

1915
Army Form C. 2118.

Appendix A

WAR DIARY
or
INTELLIGENCE SUMMARY.
(Erase heading not required.)

Hour, Date, Place.	Summary of Events and Information.	Remarks and references to Appendices
Jan 11th FESTUBERT	Marched back to BETHUNE where hot drinks were ready for officers & men —	
Jan 12th	Entrained at 1.20 AM and reached billets at PRESSANT PALFART & LIVOSSART at 7.30 AM.	
	Casualties -	
	British Ranks.	
	L/T.D. OWEN JONES. Wounded.	
	Indian Ranks.	
	Killed.	
	Jemadar - SHAM SINGH.	
	No 2052 - 47th UMED SHAH - C Sqn	
	" 2149 L/Dfr BAKHTAWAR Singl. A Sqn	
	" 2773 S. SAUTA SINGH - A Sqn	
	" 2978 " NUR KHAN - C "	
	" 3032 - L Dfr ABDUL AZIZ KHAN - C "	
	" 3091 - Sow. FATEH MD D Sqn	
	Total. 7.	
	Indian Ranks.	
	Wounded.	
	No 2706 - Sow. SUMMAN Singl. A Sqn	
	" 2880 - " AYAN Singh "	
	2426 - " UTTAM Singh "	
	" 2870 - " GULMOHAMED C	
	" 3420 - " BAHADUR KHAN C	
	2047 L.D. MAHAMED KHAN C	
	" 22 - S. WARIATM Singh A	
	61 " BASUL " A	
	2607 L.D. DASUNDA Singh A	
	1906 " BISHAN Singh A	
	3048 " AMIR SHAH B	
	2496 JELLA JHAB B	12 Wounded

P6

Army Form C. 2118.

Appendix A.

1915

WAR DIARY
or
INTELLIGENCE SUMMARY.

(Erase heading not required.)

Instructions regarding War Diaries and Intelligence Summaries are contained in F.S. Regs., Part II, and the Staff Manual respectively. Title pages will be prepared in manuscript.

Hour, Date, Place.	Summary of Events and Information.	Remarks and references to Appendices
	British Officers present.	
	Lt. Col. F. F. Rooms — Comdt.	
	Capt. H.A. Aucher — Adjut.	
	Lt. M.E. Parnall — Off. in charge of Machine Guns.	
	Major E.A. Fagan — Comdt. C. Sqdn.	
	Major M.H. Green — " A "	
	Capt. H.M. Davison — " D "	
	Capt. A.W. Gwin Jones — " B "	
	Capt. M.M. Carpendale — Comdy. B. "	
	Capt. Allen 28th Cav. — " A "	
	Lt. F.D. Gwin Jones — " C "	
	Capt. K.G. Campbell Munro — M.S. Medical Officer.	
	Interpreters.	
	Mr. Woodcock.	
	Mons. Renyaud.	

Gulab Singh & Sons, Calcutta.—No. 22 Army C.—5-8-14—1,07,000.

P.7.
Army Form C. 2118.

1915

WAR DIARY
or
INTELLIGENCE SUMMARY.
(Erase heading not required.)

Appendix – A.

Instructions regarding War Diaries and Intelligence Summaries are contained in F. S. Regs., Part II, and the Staff Manual respectively. Title pages will be prepared in manuscript.

Hour, Date, Place.	Summary of Events and Information.	Remarks and references to Appendices
	Strength of Regt.	Copy of Orders by Major Genl. F. STAPFSHAWE Comm. I.C Divn 16 Jan. 1915.
	10. B. Officers 3 O.R. Rank & file.	
	1. Med. Officer	No 4. The G.O.C. I.C. Divn wishes to express his appreciation of the gallant conduct of the British & Indian Officers mentioned below:-
	9. Interpreter.	
	Indian Officers.	
		84/Jan 10th Capt F. H. ALLARDICE
	Total admitted into hospital from front line.	36/Jacob's Horse provided men who have been admitted under heavy fire. R.I.P.
	2 B.Os (Major Fagan, Capt Alley) Capt Hugh Gore, Capt Sanders J.P. Passed and apptd Jnl.	
	75 Non Men —	
		mentioned in Sirdr's orders
	Capt. H.A. Allardice to General Conduct:-	
		mentioned in Regimental orders
	Risaldar SALEL KHAN.	
	Dfdr. POISHEN SINGH.	
	Dfdr. SAIYID HUSSAIN.	
	2934. Sr. G. HULAM Mʰᵈ Kʰ	
	2853. " SHER Mʰᵈ Kʰ 3091. Sr. FATEH MAHK (killed in action)	
	2984. " ABDUL MAJID Kʰ	
		R.I.P

Serial No. 112.

WAR DIARY

36th Jacobs Horse.

From 1st February 1915 to 28th February 1915

P.14

Army Form C. 2118.

1915

WAR DIARY of 36ᶠ JACOB'S HORSE.

or

INTELLIGENCE SUMMARY.

(Erase heading not required.)

Instructions regarding War Diaries and Intelligence Summaries are contained in F. S. Regs., Part II, and the Staff Manual respectively. Title pages will be prepared in manuscript.

Remarks and references to Appendices

No 38 ...
G's Office ....
I.E. Force
S. Sect
Passed to ....
on 5-3-15

Hour, Date, Place.	Summary of Events and Information.	
Feb 1ˢᵗ PREDEFIN. PALFART & LIVOSSART.	Billets. Regᵗ held in readiness – Snow having slightly	P.S.R
Feb 2ⁿᵈ "	Billets. Divisional Staff Ride – Rain & wind. Brigade in waiting	P.S.R
Feb 3ʳᵈ "	Billets. Brigade Exercise – Fine & warm –	R.S.R
Feb 4ᵗʰ "	Billets – Regimental Exercise – Fine & warm –	R.S.R
Feb 5ᵗʰ "	Divisional Exercise – Fine & warm –	R.S.R
Feb 6ᵗʰ "	Billets. Brigade night operations & exercise – Fine	R.S.R
Feb 7ᵗʰ "	Billets.	R.S.R
Feb 8ᵗʰ "	Billets. Brigade in training from 8 A.M. Fine	R.S.R

P. 15.

1915 WAR DIARY of 36th JACOBS' HORSE Army Form C. 2118.

INTELLIGENCE SUMMARY.

Hour, Date, Place.	Summary of Events and Information.	Remarks and references to Appendices
PREDEFIN. PALFART & LIVOSSART. Feb. 9th	Billets. Brigade out of "waiting" 8 A.M. Regt. took part in a Divisional Exercise – very stormy & rainy.	P.S.R.
Feb 10th " "	Billets. Frost last night, warm day.	P.S.R.
Feb 11th " "	Billets – Brigade Parade – Fine.	P.S.R.
Feb 12th " "	Billets. The Regiment (less Brigade) marched past in column of Half-sections. H.R.H. The Prince of Wales at FEBVIN. Snowy, cold day.	P.S.R.
Feb. 13th " "	Billets. Inspection of A & B Sqn Arms & horses by S.V.O. B'de. Night Operations – Rainy, showers of hail at intervals, muddy.	P.S.R.
Feb 14th " "	Rode in evening from 8 A.M. Halfayale, rain squalls. Lieut. The Hon'ble R.A. ADDINGTON 26th L Con. is appointed Sqn M.V. Officer in Charge Regimental Transport from 11.2.1915" wie 2nd M.E. PARNELL Hawkins Regt	P.S.R.

P. 16

1915
WAR DIARY of 36th JACOB'S HORSE   Army Form C. 2118.

or

INTELLIGENCE SUMMARY.

(Erase heading not required.)

Hour, Date, Place.	Summary of Events and Information.	Remarks and references to Appendices
PREDEFIN, PALFART & LIVOSSART. Feb. 15th	Billets.	Fine. R&R
Feb. 16th " "	"	The Regiment took part in a Divisional Exercise. Fine. R&R
Feb. 17th " "	Capt. F.R. FARQUHAR, Capt. C.H. KIRKWOOD 23rd Cav. & 2 L.O.s & 86 rank+file joined as R- in forcements. These men chiefly from 35th SCINDE HORSE. Very rainy - R&R
Feb. 18th " "	Billets.	Rainy R&R
Feb. 19th " " "	C. O's of Regiments took part in a Divisional Staff Ride.	R&R
Feb. 20th " "	Billets. Orders received for the Bde. to be in a state of readiness tomorrow at 4 hours notice. Order re duty troops cancelled. Rainy R&R
Feb. 21st	Billets.	R&R

P 17

1915 WAR DIARY of 36ʳᵈ JACOB'S HORSE or INTELLIGENCE SUMMARY.

Army Form C. 2118.

(Erase heading not required.)

Hour, Date, Place.	Summary of Events and Information.	Remarks and references to Appendices
PREDEFIN, PALFART & LIVOSSART. Dat. ser Feb. 23ʳᵈ	Billets.	R.R.
23ʳᵈ "	Regt took part in a divisional exercise.	Divl R.R.
24ᵗʰ "	Billets — Snowed heavily all day.	R.R.
25ᵗʰ "	Night operations.	R.R.
26ᵗʰ "	Billets — Capt H.S. STEWART 17ᵗʰ Cav. (attached) to Ammunition Column.	Alix Lindroos R.S.R.
27ᵗʰ "	Inspection of the Regiment by G.O.C. Lucknow Cav. Bde in marching order.	Hand just R.R.
28ᵗʰ "	Billets.	morn spine R.R.

WAR DIARY

36th Jacobs Horse.

From 1st March 1915 to 31st March 1915

1915

WAR DIARY of 36th JACOBS HORSE

or INTELLIGENCE SUMMARY

Army Form C. 2118.

P 18

ADJUTANT GENERAL INDIA - 3. APR 1915 BASE OFFICE

(Erase heading not required.)

Hour, Date, Place.	Summary of Events and Information.	Remarks and references to Appendices
PREDEFIN, PALFART & LIVOSSART — March 1st	Billets — Fine in the morning, strong wind, snow in afternoon —	R.S.R.
" " 2nd	200 men proceeded in busses, with 200 men from each of the Regiments in the Brigade, to St VENANT — ROBECQUES to dig trenches. Fine day —	R.S.R.
March 3rd "	As above — The D.D.V.S. inspected the horses of the Regiment. Very rainy & stormy, clearing towards evening.	R.S.R.
March 4th "	As above — Wet, rainy & stormy	R.S.R
March 5th "	Billets — Rainy & stormy, mist at night	R.S.R
March 6th "	Billets — Cold, snow	R.S.R.

1915.

WAR DIARY of 36th JACOB'S HORSE. Army Form C. 2118.

INTELLIGENCE SUMMARY.

(Erase heading not required.)

Instructions regarding War Diaries and Intelligence Summaries are contained in F. S. Regs., Part II, and the Staff Manual respectively. Title pages will be prepared in manuscript.

Hour, Date, Place.	Summary of Events and Information.	Remarks and references to Appendices
PREDEFIN, PALFART & LIVOSSART. March 7th	At 3.7 P.M. received orders to move into close billets in PALFART & LIVOSSART. The movement to be carried out after dark. A & B Sqns. H.Q's. & Machine Guns moved at 8 P.M. & were in their new billets at 9.20 P.M. Cold, sleet showers.	R.S.R.
PALFART & LIVOSSART. March 8th	The Regiment remained in a state of "Immediate Readiness". Cold.	R.S.R.
PALFART & LIVOSSART March 9th	The Regiment remained in a state of Immediate Readiness. Cold, fine	R.S.R.
PALFART & LIVOSSART March 10th	The Regiment remained in a state of Immediate Readiness all day. At 10 P.M. received orders to concentrate at NEDONCHELLE Church at 4.30 A.M. 11th inst.	R.S.R.
March 11th	Marched at 3.30 A.M. & concentrated with remainder of Lucknow Cav. Bde. at NEDONCHELLE Church at 4.30 A.M. Marched to LAPUGNOY & bivouaced in the BOIS de DAMES.	R.S.R.

1915

WAR DIARY 36th JACOB'S HORSE

or

INTELLIGENCE SUMMARY.

(Erase heading not required.)

P. 20.
Army Form C. 2118.

Instructions regarding War Diaries and Intelligence Summaries are contained in F. S. Regs., Part II, and the Staff Manual respectively. Title pages will be prepared in manuscript.

Hour, Date, Place.	Summary of Events and Information.	Remarks and references to Appendices
March 12th.	The Regiment in a state of readiness from 5.30 AM – a mild warm night – commenced to rain slightly at 6 AM. Concentrated (Lucknow Cav.y Bde.) at LAPUGNOY Railway Station at 12.30 P.M. & marched to and went into billets at AUCHEL reaching there at 1.20 P.M. Fine day	P.S.R.
March 13th. AUCHEL.	Remained in a state of readiness in billets. Men have baths in the mine bath rooms. Fine	P.S.R.
March 14th. AUCHEL.	Received orders for the Bde. to concentrate at the Church in AUCHEL at 1. AM. to march to billets in a new area. The Regiment went into billets at FEBVIN at 5 AM 15 but.	P.S.R.
March 15th. FEBVIN.	Billets - arrived at 5. AM. Fine	P.S.R.

P. 21.
Army Form C. 2118.

1915

WAR DIARY of 36th JACOB's
or
~~INTELLIGENCE SUMMARY.~~

(Erase heading not required.)

Instructions regarding War Diaries and Intelligence Summaries are contained in F. S. Regs., Part II, and the Staff Manual respectively. Title pages will be prepared in manuscript.

Hour, Date, Place.	Summary of Events and Information.	Remarks and references to Appendices
FEBVIN. March 16th.	In billets. - Reg't at 2 hours notice. Fine.	RER
FEBVIN. March 17th.	In billets. Capt. C.H. KIRKWOOD. 23rd Cav.(attd) appointed to Divisional Ammunition Column. Fine.	RER
March 18th.	The Indian Cavalry Corps inspected by G.O.C. Corps near RELY. After the inspection marched into new billets as under— A Sq'n ⎫ ⎬ in LIETTRES B Sq'n ⎭ C Sq'n ⎫ ⎬ in LINGHEM. D Sq'n ⎭ Machine Guns - Fine but chilly.	RER
LIETTRES & LINGHEM. March 19th.	Under orders of 6 hours notice. - Showered in the night. Snowshowers all day.	RER
do. do. March 20th.	Billets. Men had baths at FLECHINELLE Mines.	RER

Gulab Singh & Sons, Calcutta—No. 22 Army C.—5-8-14—1,07,000.

1915

WAR DIARY of 36th JACOB'S HORSE.

or

INTELLIGENCE SUMMARY.

(Erase heading not required.)

Army Form C. 2118.
P. 22

Instructions regarding War Diaries and Intelligence Summaries are contained in F. S. Regs., Part II, and the Staff Manual respectively. Title pages will be prepared in manuscript.

Hour, Date, Place.	Summary of Events and Information.	Remarks and references to Appendices
LIETTRES, N. LINGHEM March 21st	Billets - Routine work.	Fine. R.R
" March 22nd	Billets - Routine work.	Fine - frost. R.R
" March 23rd	Billets. Routine work.	Fine frost then rain & afternoon R.R
" March 24th	Billets. Inspection in the Field by G.O.C. 13th	Rain snow. R.R
" March 25th	Billets. Routine work.	Rain cold. R.R
" March 26th	Billets - Routine work.	Fine cold. R.R
" March 27th	Billets - Routine work.	Fine cold. R.R
" March 28th	Billets. Routine work.	Fine cold wind. R.R
March 29th	Billets. Routine work.	Fine cold wind. R.R
March 30th	Billets. Routine work.	Fine cold wind. R.R

1915 P.23

WAR DIARY of 36th Jacob's HORSE   Army Form C. 2118.

INTELLIGENCE SUMMARY.

(Erase heading not required.)

Hour, Date, Place.	Summary of Events and Information.	Remarks and references to Appendices
LIETTRES & LINGHEM. March 31st	Routine — Fine weather	PeR

121/5584

General No 112

Mer 6/5

WAR DIARY
OF
36th Jacob's Horse

From 1st April 1915 To 30th April 1915

T. 24

1915

WAR DIARY of 36th JACOB'S HORSE Army Form C. 2118.

or

INTELLIGENCE SUMMARY.

(Erase heading not required.)

Instructions regarding War Diaries and Intelligence Summaries are contained in F. S. Regs., Part II, and the Staff Manual respectively. Title pages will be prepared in manuscript.

Hour, Date, Place.	Summary of Events and Information.	Remarks and references to Appendices
LIETTRES & LINGHEM. April 1st.	Billets	Fine. F.S.R.
do. do. April 2nd. "	Billets.	Fine. F.S.R.
do. do. April 3rd. "	Billets. Capt. A.M. FORTEATH. (at Depot) to be Officiating 1st Sq. Comdr vice Major E.A. FAGAN Officiating 2nd in Command with effect from 1st January, 1915. Capt. E.B. MAUNSELL, 35. Horse attached to Regiment	Divnl Order. No 1 (11) d/3.4.15 F.S.R. Divnl Order No 2. 11 d/3.4.15 F.S.R. Fine
do. do. April 4th.	Billets.	Fine then Raining. F.S.R.
do. do. April 5th	Billets.	Fine then Rain. F.S.R.

1915 P 25

WAR DIARY of 36 JACOB'S HORSE.

INTELLIGENCE SUMMARY.

Army Form C. 2118.

(Erase heading not required.)

Hour, Date, Place.	Summary of Events and Information.	Remarks and references to Appendices
LIETTRES & LINGHEM. Billets. April - 6th.	Major E.A. FAGAN to officiate as 2nd in Command vice Major C.H. ALEXANDER, medically unfit, with effect from 1st January 1915. 2nd Lt A.L. GORDON-KIDD attached to Regt from 5th that. Fine then rain.	Divnl Order. No 120.-(2) d/ 6.4.1915 Divnl Order. No 120 3. iii d/ 6.4.1915. R&R.
do. do. April - 7th.	Billets. Fine then rain.	R&R.
do. do. April - 8th.	Billets. Showery.	R.&R.
do. do. April - 9th.	Billets. Showery	R.&R.

1915
P. 26.
WAR DIARY of 36 JACOB'S HORSE. Army Form C. 2118.

or

INTELLIGENCE SUMMARY.

(Erase heading not required.)

Hour, Date, Place.	Summary of Events and Information.	Remarks and references to Appendices
LIETTRES & LINGHEM. April 10th	Billets. 9 men of 35th SCINDE HORSE joined as x-interement from Base.— The Brigade Horse Show took place today in which the Regt won the following events:— Officers Jumping. Lt. Blacker (1st), Lt. Russell (2nd). Indian Officers Jumping. Jem. Bishen Singh 1st. Sowars Jumping. L.Dfr. Amar Singh 1st, Sowar Nuida Singh 2nd. Officers Chargers under 15 hds. Capt. Grenn-Jones "Brickbat". J. Officers Chargers. R.M. Muhammad Husein Khan 2nd. Section (Horsed). Merchies Gun Section 3rd.	P.S.R.
do April 11th do	Sowars Jumping Competition held today.	Fine. P.S.R.
do do April 12th	Billets.	Fine. P.S.R.

1915

WAR DIARY of 36 JACOB'S HORSE, Army Form C. 2118.

or

INTELLIGENCE SUMMARY.

(Erase heading not required.)

Instructions regarding War Diaries and Intelligence Summaries are contained in F. S. Regs., Part II, and the Staff Manual respectively. Title pages will be prepared in manuscript.

Hour, Date, Place.	Summary of Events and Information.	Remarks and references to Appendices
LIETTRES & LINGHEM. April 13th	22 days Advance hooks received. 20 f Wheeled - also A.T. Carts for carrying horse rugs. 73 dt Transport Rents hired.	Fine. P&R
do do April 14th T.	Practice in night operations - attack at dawn.	Fine. R&R.
do do April 15th	The Division marched past certain newspaper Correspondents at HURTERISE. The following Yeomanry Officers joined today. Capt. J.F.M. ROBINSON. East Riding Yeo? " T.C. TROLLOPE. LINCOLNSHIRE Yeo." Lieut J. ROBERTSON. SCOTTISH HORSE.	Fine. P&R.
do do April 16th	Divisional Staff Tour.	

1915
WAR DIARY of 36th JACOB'S HORSE P.28
Army Form C. 2118.

WAR DIARY
or
INTELLIGENCE SUMMARY.
(Erase heading not required.)

Hour, Date, Place.		Summary of Events and Information.	Remarks and references to Appendices
LIETTRES v LINGHEM April 17th	Billets		True. RSR.
do. do. April 18th	Billets		True. RSR.
do. do. April 19th	Billets		True. RSR.
do. do. April 20th	Billets		True. RSR
do. do. April 21st	Billets		True. RSR
do. do. April 22nd	Billets		True. RSR
do. do. April 23rd	Billets		True. RSR

P 29

1915 -

WAR DIARY of the 36- JACOB'S HORSE. Army Form C. 2118.

or

INTELLIGENCE SUMMARY.

(Erase heading not required.)

Instructions regarding War Diaries and Intelligence Summaries are contained in F. S. Regs., Part II, and the Staff Manual respectively. Title pages will be prepared in manuscript.

Hour, Date, Place.	Summary of Events and Information.	Remarks and references to Appendices
LIETTRÈS-LINGHEM. April - 24ᵗʰ	At 10 A.M. Received orders for the Regiment to be ready to move at two hours notice. - At 5. P.M. Received orders for the Regᵗ to march at once to Eecouenents	R.S.R.
OXELAERE. OXELAERE π April. 25ᵗʰ	At ESTREÉ-BLANCHE marched from ESTREÉ-BLANCHE with mounted of Brigade. The Regʳ marched from ESTREÉ-BLANCHE 7.15 P.M. & went into billets in the communes of OXELAERE. S.ᵗ CASSEL at 4 A.M. - rain heavily from midnight on to morning.	
do -	Spent the day in billets; regiment remaining in a state of instant readiness. Fine in afternoon	R.S.R.
OXELAERE. Ap. 26ᵗʰ OXELAERE.	Billets - Regᵗ - remains in a state of instant readiness. Fine	R.S.R.
OXELAERE. Ap. 27ᵗʰ	Billets. Regᵗ - Remains in a state of instant readiness. Fine -	R.S.R.
OXELAERE. Ap. 28ᵗʰ	Billets. Received orders for the Brigade to concentrate at crossroads close to Brigade H.Qrs at 11.30 A.M. Marched via CASSEL and STEENVOORDE to Sᵗ JEAN-TER-BIEZEN when the Regᵗ	R.S.R.

1915

P 30

WAR DIARY of the 36th JACOB'S HORSE P. 30.

or

INTELLIGENCE SUMMARY. Army Form C. 2118.

(Erase heading not required.)

Hour, Date, Place	Summary of Events and Information	Remarks and references to Appendices
28th April Con td	Went in to billets for the night in some farms between St JEAN-TER-BIEZEN and POPERINGHE. Fine.	P.S.R.
ST JEAN-TER-BIEZEN. 29th April -	Billets. Regt remained in a state of instant readiness. 2nd Lt E.N. WALDRON. I.A. Reserve of Officers reported his arrival & is appointed Regtl Transport Officer. Fine fine & warm.	R.P.
ST JEAN-TER-BIEZEN. 30th April.	Billets. Regt remained in a state of instant readiness. Thick mist in the early morning. Fine warm day	P.S.R.

R.G. Browne Clayton
2nd Lt 36 Jacob's Horse.
Com. 1.5.1915.

10 SH/666/a

WAR DIARY

36th Jacob's Horse.

From 1st May 1945 to 31st May 1945

P. 31/-

1915
WAR DIARY of 36 JACOB'S HORSE
or INTELLIGENCE SUMMARY.
(Erase heading not required.)

Army Form C. 2118.

A.G. OFFICE. 3rd ECH. BASE
No. 12254 W.D.
4 JUN. 1915
INDIAN SECTION

Instructions regarding War Diaries and Intelligence Summaries are contained in F. S. Regs., Part II and the Staff Manual respectively. Title pages will be prepared in manuscript.

Hour, Date, Place	Summary of Events and Information	Remarks and references to Appendices
ST JEAN-TER-BIEZEN. May 1st	Billets - At 11.30 P.M. Received orders for the Brigade to move to its previous billets and to concentrate at crossroads N½R of WARANDEBECK at 6 A.M. Fine day, warm.	R.O.
OXELAERE May 2nd	Arrived at our old billets in the OXELAERE commune at 9.30 A.M. & went into our old billets. Fine day.	R.S.O.
OXELAERE May 3rd	Billets. Fine day, wind cold.	R.O.
OXELAERE May 4th	Billets. Received orders to march at 2 A.M. 5th inst. Rain storm evening - fine afterwards.	R.O.R.
MARTHES-HAM-BLESSY May 5th	Arrived at MARTHES at 6.30 A.M. & went into billets as under:- H.d qrs. ⎫ Machine Guns ⎬ MARTHES. C Sqn. ⎭ B Sqn - HAM. A & D Sqn - BLESSY. Fine warm.	R.O.R.

1915
P 32

WAR DIARY of 30th JACOBSHORSE
or
INTELLIGENCE SUMMARY

Army Form C. 2118.

(Erase heading not required.)

Instructions regarding War Diaries and Intelligence Summaries are contained in F. S. Regs., Part II. and the Staff Manual respectively. Title pages will be prepared in manuscript.

Hour, Date, Place	Summary of Events and Information	Remarks and references to Appendices
MARTHES-HAM-BLESSY. May 6th	Billet.	Fine - warm - RcR
do. do. May 7th	Billet	Rain afternoon xxx U RcR warm F.59°/0 am
do - do May 8th	Billet - Orders received at 9.35 PM for the Regiment to be ready to march at 2 hours notice from 5AM. Gt/hst. Saddles to men "B" Echelon to be brigaded at MAMETZ & baggage to be dumped there under a Guard of 3 men. The supply wagons to be employed for other purposes. Fine & warm	RcR
do. do. May 9th	Billets. Still at 2 hours notice. Capn A. MARSHALL 28th L. Cav. attd. - posted to the Flying Corps. 2nd Lt. A.L. GORDON-KIDD I.A.R.O. attd. allot to the Amm.n Column - Capt. C.H. KIRKWOOD 23rd Cav "Rejoined the rgt from the Ammunition Column - Cold Northerly Wind - Fine	RcR

(73989) W4141—463. 400,000. 9/14. H.&J.Ltd. Forms/C. 2118/10.

1915

WAR DIARY of 36th JACOB'S HORSE. P 33

or

INTELLIGENCE SUMMARY.

(Erase heading not required.)

Army Form C. 2118.

Instructions regarding War Diaries and Intelligence Summaries are contained in F. S. Regs., Part II. and the Staff Manual respectively. Title pages will be prepared in manuscript.

Hour, Date, Place	Summary of Events and Information	Remarks and references to Appendices
MARTHES, HAM & BLESSY. May - 10th	Billets. At 2 hours notice. Fine - warmer.	R&R
do. do. May - 11th	Billets. Adopted a blue & yellow band on shoulder as a distinguishing mark. At 2 hours notice. Fine - warmer.	R&R
do. do. May - 12th	Billets. At 2 hours notice. At 8.45 P.M. received orders to be ready to move at 4 hours notice. Cloudy -	R&R
do. do. May. 13th	Billets. Rained during night. Capt. C. H. KIRKWOOD 23rd Cav. a.Rd. transferred to 3rd SKINNERS HORSE. Rain.	R.S.R.
do. do. May 14th	Billets. Rain.	R&R
May. 15th	Billets. Fine.	R&R
May 16	Billets. This evening received 32 remounts. Also 5 limbered wagons Fine. Issued with Mules for "A" Echelon viz 1 M.C. 0, 4 10 A.G.C. wagons as drivers	R&R

(73989) W4141—463. 400,000. 9/14. H.&J.Ltd. Forms/C. 2118/10.

1915

WAR DIARY of 36 JACOB'S HORSE.
or
INTELLIGENCE SUMMARY.
(Erase heading not required.)

P. 34 Army Form C. 2118.

Instructions regarding War Diaries and Intelligence Summaries are contained in F.S. Regs., Part II. and the Staff Manual respectively. Title pages will be prepared in manuscript.

Hour, Date, Place	Summary of Events and Information	Remarks and references to Appendices
MARTHES, HAM & BLESSY. May - 17th	At 1.40 P.M. received orders to be ready to move. At 4. P.M. received orders to march at once at a trot to the Brigade Rendez-vous at the CHAMP DE MANOEUVRES west of AIRE. Enroute received orders that the Brigade was moving via LAMBRES, STHILAIRE LILLERS & HAUT RIEUX. At 8.30 P.M. reached REVEILLON and went into bivouac there - Pouring rain - This morning 5 A.T. Carts & 10 Brab'n wagons turned up late Transport	P.S.R
REVEILLON. May. 18th BURBURE.	At 12.30 P.M. received orders to march to BURBURE at 2.30 P.M. and go into billets there - Arrived BURBURE at 3.30 P.M. Rain & mist -	P.S.R
BURBURE. May - 19th	Billets" At 12.30. noon received orders to march at 1.50 P.M. and return to our old billets at MARTHES, HAM & BLESSY. Reached there at 4.30 P.M. and squadrons went into their old billets. At 6. P.M. received orders to be in readiness at 4 hours notice. Rain & mist.	P.S.R

1915   P. 35

WAR DIARY of 30th JACOB'S HORSE.
or
INTELLIGENCE SUMMARY.

Army Form C. 2118.

(Erase heading not required.)

Instructions regarding War Diaries and Intelligence Summaries are contained in F.S. Regs., Part II. and the Staff Manual respectively. Title pages will be prepared in manuscript.

Hour, Date, Place	Summary of Events and Information	Remarks and references to Appendices
MARTHES, HAMUBLESSY Billets - May. 20th	1 N.C.O. A.S.C. arrived last night the i/c charge of A.S.C. Drivers. Fine	R.S.R.
do - do Billets - May. 21st	Fine	R.S.R.
do - do Billets - May. 22nd	1 Farrier A.S.C. Joined. Fine	R.S.R.
do - do Billets - May. 23rd	Fine	R.S.R.
do - do Billets - May. 24th	6 Riding horses received from Mobile Vet. Section. Fine	R.S.R.
do - do Billets - May. 25th	Risaldar AZAM ALI (22nd (av.) & 6 men joined from Dwt. Amm Column. Fine	R.S.R.
do - do May. 26th	Received news that the Division would move to CASSELS to-morrow.	

(73989) W4141—463. 400,000. 9/14. H.&J.Ltd. Forms/C. 2118/10.

P. 36.

1915

WAR DIARY of 3rd JACOBS HORSE
or
INTELLIGENCE SUMMARY.

(Erase heading not required.)

Army Form C. 2118.

Hour, Date, Place	Summary of Events and Information	Remarks and references to Appendices
217. MARTHES, HAM & BLESSY. 27. May - OXELAERE. 12.45.P.M.	Marched at 8.30 a.m arrived OXELAERE 12.45 P.M. Orders received at 6.30 P.M for the Reg't & "B" Echelon to march at 6.30 A.M to L'ERKLESBRUGGE. "A" Echelon to BRANDHOEK.	P.S.R
OXELAERE 28th May - L'ERKLESBRUGGE.	"A" Echelon - marched at 5.A.M - Reg't marched at 6.A.M - arrived at L'ERKLESBRUGGE at 9.30 A.M. 14 B.O.S. 11 I.O.S. 4 other Ranks. 246 Horses Ranks & onwards at 2.P.M & arrived at BRANDHOEK (VLAMERTINGE) at 2.P.M - & went into Shelter into there - Remainder of Reg't remained in fields at with horses at L'ERKLESBRUGGE.	P.S.R
BRANDHOEK 29th May -	In shelter huts. J/M" R.E. ROOME returned from leave - Strength now 15 B.O.S - Major Gen'l ALLENB'y inspected the Reg't. Comg.R "Camp"	P.S.R
BRANDHOEK 30th May -	In shelter huts. Remainder of Reg't at L'ERKLESBRUGGE. Majors Cap'n FARQUHAR & Cap'n ROBINSON reconnoitred the ground towards HOOGE -	

P. 37

1915
WAR DIARY of 36 JACOB'S HORSE
or
INTELLIGENCE SUMMARY.

Army Form C. 2118.

Hour, Date, Place	Summary of Events and Information	Remarks and references to Appendices
BRANDHOEK. May 31st	Sheikh huts - Kurainder of Regt al L'ERKLESBRUGGE. Major FAGAN, Capt. DAVIDSON, FARQUHAR MAUNSELL, GAVIN-JONES PARNELL, Ress. SANTSINGH, SADIKMAHOMED, KHAN MUHAMMAD KHAN, Jem.dr MAQBULSHAH went into the Trenches South of HOOGE for instruction tonight. BRANDHOEK. R.S. Towne Lt. Col. May 31st 1915. Comdg. 36 Jacobs Horse Com No: JH/834/a	R.S.R.

Serial No. 112

121/6128

WAR DIARY
OF
36th Jacobs' Horse.

From 1st June 1915 To 30th June 1915.

1915 *36th JACOB'S HORSE* P.38. Army Form C. 2118.

WAR DIARY or INTELLIGENCE SUMMARY

Hour, Date, Place	Summary of Events and Information	Remarks and references to Appendices
June 1st — BRANDHOEK —	H.Qrs. B.Os. 15, I.Os. 11, B.O. other Ranks 4. I.O.R. 265.	
L'ERKLESBRUGGE —	Remainder of Regt and horses —	
6.15 P.M.	A working party of 2 B.Os. 2 N.Os. & 100 men was ordered up as a carrying party of R.E. stores to take the stores up to the Chateau just north of HOOGE. Lieut. J.K.Heut W.R. ADDINGTON & ROBERTSON went in charge. (Capt. CARPENDALE, ALLARDICE, 2nd. OWEN-JONES, Capt. ROBINSON, and Capt. MUNRO I.M.S. TROLLOPE (2nd L't ROBERTSON assisting the transfer of the trucks after taking the working party up). 2nd L't WALDRON took up the Transport of the K.D.F.S. & the firing line — Capt. CARBENDALE joined in completion of M.G. Course.	PER R.I.R
June 2nd — BRANDHOEK	Majors FAGAN & Capt. K.M. HUNSELL proceeded to L'ERKLESBRUGGE. H.Qrs. B.O. 14, N.O. 11. B.O.R. 4. I.O.R. 266. 3 horses wounded last night by shrapnel between YPRES & HOOGE. 1 man of above working party reported missing supposed blown — been killed by a shell. 6/6. P.M. regiment was ordered to be in readiness twenty minutes by in support of 3rd Cavalry Division.	R.I.R

WAR DIARY of 36th JAC'BS HORSE
or INTELLIGENCE SUMMARY.

Army Form C. 2118.

1915

(Erase heading not required.)

Hour, Date, Place	Summary of Events and Information	Remarks and references to Appendices
June 3rd BRANDHOEK.	The Regiment continued in a state of readiness. At 7.30 PM received orders to move up at once in support East of YPRES. On marching through YPRES the Reg't came into contact with enormous gas fumes shells, in the vicinity of the CLOTH HALL. The men put on masks, but one man was not affected seriously and some others slightly and got indoors had Capt. MUNRO I.M.S. who was attending those affected — On reaching the SALLY PORT East of YPRES received verbal orders for 3 Sqdns to advance and occupy the "YEOMAN'S POST" (which is roughly 1100× S.W of HODGE × 1200× N.W of HILL 60) one Sqdn to go with 29 Lancers & occupy the trenches known as G.H.Q. line South of the MENIN Road — A, B & D Sqdns ... reached YEOMAN'S Post shortly after midnight × from ... during at the old Tench farm buildings. The orders being not to show themselves on any account but to be ready to turn off any given in support of regiment. Casualties: R.N° 2582 Dafadar DHULEEP SINGH, gassed R.N°3121 L/Dfr. SAMANDAR KHAN, bullet wound —	App° I. Officers present ~~C~~ Lt/Col T. E. ROYNE, Com'd'g Capt. H. ALLARDICE. Adj'd Capt. A.C. MUNRO. I.M.S "A" Sqdn Major W.G.K. GREEN Lt/The Hon'ble R.A. ADDINGTON (2nd.C.CIO) "B" Sqdn Capt. A. GAVIN-JONES Capt. M.M. CARPENDALE "C" Sqdn Capt. F.R. FARQUHAR 2nd Lt. E.M. WALDRON J.A.R. Oa 11th E. RIDINAY's Adj'd A Eckstein D. Sqdn Capt. H.M. DAVIDSON Capt. J.F.M. ROBINSON Lt. R. OWEN-JONES Machine guns Lt. M.E. PARNELL
YEOMAN'S POST. (midnight)		

P 40 –

Army Form C. 2118.

1915

WAR DIARY of 36th JACOB'S HORSE
or
INTELLIGENCE SUMMARY.
(Erase heading not required.)

Instructions regarding War Diaries and Intelligence Summaries are contained in F.S. Regs., Part II. and the Staff Manual respectively. Title pages will be prepared in manuscript.

Hour, Date, Place	Summary of Events and Information	Remarks and references to Appendices
June 3rd Cont'd	"C" Sqn. Made their trenches at 1 AM (without). No incident.	P.C.R.
June 4th YEOMAN'S POST.	A, B & D Sqns remained concealed the whole day without incident, beyond being under two aimed overseas rifle fire three times of the salient. In the evening received orders to support the Brigade when placed at the disposal of B. Genl. HELY-HUTCHINSON. The night was spent in improving the defences of the POST which had been built under a convenient un-aimed rifle fire. Stood to arms at 9 AM till 2:48 AM. Remained concealed the whole day. At 5 P.M. received orders that the 3rd (Momentary) Bde Cav R. Casualties. Reg'l No 3402 ALIVAR KHAN - wounded. A few shells fell on "C" Sqn in the morning - no casualties. The night of 4th - 5th spent in improving the trenches.	P.C.P.
G.H.Q Line -		
June 5th YEOMAN'S POST	A, B & D Sqns remained concealed the whole day. At 5 P.M. received orders to march back to our former huts & trenches. A Echelon arrived at 10.30 P.M - remainder of Sq. at 10.40 P.M. Left the POST at 10.35 P.M & reached VLAMMERTINGHE at 1 A.M. (5th - 15 mi). "C" Sqn joined en route. No incidents. The march was along the roads early.	App'd Order No 2. P.C.P.

P. 41

Army Form C. 2118.

WAR DIARY of 36th JACOBS HORSE
or INTELLIGENCE SUMMARY
1915

(Erase heading not required.)

Instructions regarding War Diaries and Intelligence Summaries are contained in F.S. Regs., Part II. and the Staff Manual respectively. Title pages will be prepared in manuscript.

Hour, Date, Place	Summary of Events and Information	Remarks and references to Appendices
BRANDHOEK June 6th L'ERKLESBRUGGE	In shelter. Horses & remainder of Regt. Fine & very hot.	R.R
June 7th do	do - Camps in vicinity shelled in the vicinity.	P.S.R.
June 8th do	Brig hunches Blake born in at BRANDHOEK. no -	do - slight rain in evening. very hot. R.R
June 9th do	Capt Esq CARPENDALE, ROBINSON, TROLLOPE, ROBERTSON, proceeded to L'ERKLESBRUGGE to be relieved by Jnr BLACKER & GORDON-KIDD.	Rained during night. R.R
June 10th do	Camps in vicinity shelled -	Fine - warm. R.R.
June 11th	Camp shelled at 9 P.M. the Regiment moved into fields in the vicinity until shelling ceased - VLAMMERTINGHE church hit by Fire bomb. Incendiary shells	R.R

(73989) W4141—463. 400,000. 9/14. H.&J.Ltd. Forms/C. 2118/10.

P.42.

1915.

WAR DIARY ₉ 36ᴱ JACOB'S HORSE
INTELLIGENCE SUMMARY
(Erase heading not required.)

Army Form C. 2118.

Instructions regarding War Diaries and Intelligence Summaries are contained in F. S. Regs., Part II. and the Staff Manual respectively. Title pages will be prepared in manuscript.

Hour, Date, Place	Summary of Events and Information	Remarks and references to Appendices
BRANDHOEK. June 12ᵀʰ	Camp shelled at 5.30 A.M. - Moved into fields until 7 A.M. when Shelling ceased. (3 men killed & 4 wounded amongst other Regiments formation) The rest of the day passed without incident - Fine -	P.S.R.
do. June 13	Went into the trenches prepared by us at 6 P.M. & bivouacked there this night - No shelling of Camps however - BM/65 Received orders to return to L'ERKLESBRUGGE.	P.S.R.
do. June 14ᵀʰ	Marched to BRANDHOEK & moved from there to L'ERKLESBRUGGE Received orders to Entrain for the billetting area tomorrow.	R.S.R.
June 15ᵗʰ	Marched at 8 A.M. & reached area at 1.30 P.M. Found MARTHES occupied by Transport. Billetted in BLESSY (A.B.D.Sqdn. M.guns & Headquarters. Very congested) C Sqdn at HAM. Received information that No 2571.S. Broken Singh reported missing on 1ˢᵗ that had been received into Hospital wounded -	R.S.R.
June 16ᵀʰ BLESSY & HAM.	British. On 4 hours notice from 6 A.M.	R.S.R.

1915
P43

WAR DIARY of 36th JACOB'S HORSE.
or
INTELLIGENCE SUMMARY.

(Erase heading not required.)

Army Form C. 2118.

Hour, Date, Place	Summary of Events and Information	Remarks and references to Appendices
June 17th MARTHES, HAM & BLESSY.	Hd qrs, Machine Guns, & D Sqdn moved into billets at MARTHES. Remainder of Regt. remained in their present billets. Fine.	R.u.R.
June 18th do. do.	Billets. Bde at 5 hours notice, Units at 4 hours notice - Fine.	R.u.R
June 19th do. do.	Billets. Fine.	P.S.u.R
June 20th do. do.	Billets. Fine.	R.u.R.
June 21st do. do.	Billets - Fine.	R.u.R
June 22nd do. do.	Billets. C.O. 2nd i/c dx M. Gun Officer attended a short Course in Machine Guns at WISQUES. Fine	R.u.R
June 23rd do. do. do.	do - do - Rain in aftn.	R.u.R.

WAR DIARY of 36ᵗʰ JACOB'S HORSE. P. 44.
Army Form C. 2118.

or

INTELLIGENCE SUMMARY.

(Erase heading not required.)

Hour, Date, Place	Summary of Events and Information	Remarks and references to Appendices
MARTHES, HAM & BLESSY. June 24ᵗʰ	Billets. R. No 2501 L. Dfr AMER SINGH won the jumping competition to Sowars at the Corps Horse Show held at ESTRÉE BLANCHE to-day.	R&R.
do. do. June 25ᵗʰ	Billets.	Cloudy, showers in afternoon. R&R.
do. do. June 26ᵗʰ	Billets.	Rain in afternoon. R&R.
do. do. June 27ᵗʰ	Billets.	Fine. R&R.
do. do. June 28ᵗʰ	Billets.	Fine then heavy showers R&R
do. do. June 29ᵗʰ	Billets.	Showery R&R
do. do. June 30ᵗʰ	Billets.	Fine. R&R

Fine. T. E. Hogue Lt Col.
July 1·19 Comm. 36ᵗʰ Jacob's Horse.

Serial No. 112.

121/6502

WAR DIARY
OF

36th Jacob's Horse.

From 1st July 1915 To 31st July 1915

P 45
Army Form C. 2118.

WAR DIARY of 36 JACOB'S HORSE
1915
INTELLIGENCE SUMMARY.
(Erase heading not required.)

Instructions regarding War Diaries and Intelligence Summaries are contained in F.S. Regs., Part II. and the Staff Manual respectively. Title pages will be prepared in manuscript.

Hour, Date, Place	Summary of Events and Information	Remarks and references to Appendices
MARTHES, HAM & BLESSY. July 1st	Billets.	Fine. R&R.
do. do. July 2nd	Billets.	Fine. R&R
do. do. July 3rd	Billets	Fine R&R
do. do. July 4th	Billets.	Hot/Thu R&R
do. do. July 5th	Billets. Capt. H. ALLARDICE appointed Staff Captain SIALKOTE Cav. Bde - inspected his departure on this date.	
do. do. July 6th	Billets. The Crown Prince of SERVIA accompanied by Gnls RIMINGTON, FANSHAWE & TASKER visited the Regiment and went round some of the Squadrons in their lines & billets.	
do. do. July 7th	A sandy strength 320 2m turned to enlarged MAMETZ to dig trenches in the vicinity of ZELOBES (VIEILLE CHAPELLE). Major FAGAN Commanded the party - British Officers - Major GORDON, Capt CARPENDALE, Capt ROBINSON, Capt MUNRO LMS - Lt BLACKER, Lt CORDON-NIDD	

P.46
Army Form C. 2118.

WAR DIARY of 36th JACOB'S HORSE.
or
INTELLIGENCE SUMMARY.

(Erase heading not required.)

Instructions regarding War Diaries and Intelligence Summaries are contained in F. S. Regs., Part II. and the Staff Manual respectively. Title pages will be prepared in manuscript.

Hour, Date, Place	Summary of Events and Information	Remarks and references to Appendices
MAMETZ, HAM & BLESSY. July 8th.	The Regt. with the rest of the Indian Cavalry Corps formed up at Rombly this morning to be inspected by Lord KITCHENER. Fine	R&R.
do. do. July 9th.	Billets – Showery – Fine	R&R.
do. do. July 10th.	Billets. Fine.	R&R.
do. do. July 11th.	Billets. The cavalry returned from digging line to-day. Cloudy. Cold.	R&R.
do. do. July 12th.	Billets. Showery –	R&R.
do. do. July 13th.	Billets. Fine.	R&R.
do. do. July 14th.	Billets. Fine	R&R.

P. 47

Army Form C. 2118.

WAR DIARY of 36 JACOB'S HORSE.
or
INTELLIGENCE SUMMARY.
(Erase heading not required.)

Hour, Date, Place	Summary of Events and Information	Remarks and references to Appendices
MARTHES HAMS BLESSY. JULY 15th.	Billeb. Capth. C. F. CAHUSAC returned from the Base depôt at MARSEILLES and took up the appointment of Adjutant.	Frie RcR
do. do. July 16th do	Billeb.	Frie. RcR.
do. do. July 17th.	Billeb. A digging party, strength as under entrained at MAMETZ at 8 A.M. to dig trenches in the vicinity of FOSSE and ROUGE CROIX. 2nd Lieut ROOME (in command of the Brigade digging Party) Major GREEN Major ROBERTSON, Capth. MUNRO I.M.S. & F. OWEN-JONES. 8 subaltern officers & 150 Sabres.	Frie RcR
do. do. July 18th.	Billeb.	RcR
do. do. July 19th.	Capth. GAVIN-JONES & 10 men entrained at MAMETZ at 8 A.M. to join the digging Party at FOSSE.	RcR
do. do. July 20th.	Billeb.	RcR.

P. 48

Army Form C. 2118.

1915
WAR DIARY of 36 Jacob's Horse
or
INTELLIGENCE SUMMARY.

(Erase heading not required.)

Hour, Date, Place	Summary of Events and Information	Remarks and references to Appendices
MARTHES, HAM & BLESSY July 20th	nil.	ReR.
do. do. July 21st	Recvd. Indian Drivers from the Ammunition Column to replace A.S.C. Drivers.	ReR
do. do. July 22nd	Recvd. 1 Sergt. 15 A.S.C. Drivers returned to A.S.C.	ReR
do. do. July 23rd	nil.	ReR.
do. do. July 24th	nil.	ReR.
do. do. July 25th	nil.	ReR.
do. do. July 26th	nil.	ReR.
do. do. July 27th	nil. Digging Party returned. No casualties.	ReR.

49.

Army Form C. 2118.

1915
WAR DIARY of 36th JACOB'S HORSE.
or
INTELLIGENCE SUMMARY.
(Erase heading not required.)

Hour, Date, Place	Summary of Events and Information	Remarks and references to Appendices
MARTHES, HAM & BLESSY. July 28th	British.	Fine. P.C.R.
do do July 29th	British. 2nd Lieut A.L. GORDON-RIDD evacuated to Hospital as unlikely hurt.	Fine. R.S.R
do do July 30th	British. Lieut C.L. KERR REID I.A.R.O reported the arrival and was attached to "B" Sqn.	Fine. P.C.R
do do July 31st	British. Received orders to move to a new Billeting Area.	Fine. P.C.R.

R.G. Thomas Lt Col us
Comdg 36/Jacob Horse
Aug 1st 1915.

Serial No. 112.

12/6948

WAR DIARY
OF
36th Jacob's Horse

FROM 1st August 1915 TO 31st August 1915

1915
P.50
Army Form C. 2118.

WAR DIARY of 36th JACOB'S HORSE.
or
INTELLIGENCE SUMMARY.
(Erase heading not required.)

Hour, Date, Place	Summary of Events and Information	Remarks and references to Appendices
FRUGES. Aug 1st	Marched to FRUGES. Hot & cloudy. Slight rain in afternoon. Billets in town - men & horses in 2 fields.	P.S.R.
ECQUEMICOURT. Aug 2nd	Marched to ECQUEMICOURT today. Horses were in a field by the river - rained heavily in the evening. Capt. E.B. MAURSELL 35th Scinde Horse joined HdQrs. III Army as G.S.O. 3rd grade	P.S.R.
RIBEAUCOURT. Aug 3rd	Marched to RIBEAUCOURT today, men billeted in the village. Rained heavily last night & storms during the day.	P.S.R.
BERTEAUCOURT LesDames. Aug 4th	Marched to BERTEAUCOURT LESDAMES today & went into bivouac on meadows close to R. NIEVRE. Rained heavily in the morning. Fine afternoon.	P.S.R.
do. Aug 5th	In bivouac.	Fine. P.S.R.
do Aug 6th	In bivouac. Rained heavily during night & morning. The meadows in which horses was became a swamp. Changing billets this afternoon.	P.S.R.

1915
P 5/1.
WAR DIARY of 36 JACOB'S HORSE.
Army Form C. 2118.

or

INTELLIGENCE SUMMARY.

(Erase heading not required.)

Hour, Date, Place	Summary of Events and Information	Remarks and references to Appendices
BERTEAUCOURT-LES-DAMES. Aug 7th.	British.	Rain. R&R.
do. do.	British. A Sqdn moved into a billeting area West of the village	
HALLOYS Aug 8th.	of HALLOYS as the ground they were on became too swampy.	Heavy rain. R&R.
do. do. Aug 9th.	British.	Heavy rain. R&R.
do. do. Aug 10th.	British.	Fine. R&R
do. do. Aug 11th.	British.	Rain. R&R
do. do. Aug 12th.	British.	Rain. R&R
Aug 13th	British.	Rain in afternoon. R&R

1915

P.52

WAR DIARY of 36th JACOB'S HORSE.

Army Form C. 2118.

INTELLIGENCE SUMMARY.

(Erase heading not required.)

Hour, Date, Place	Summary of Events and Information	Remarks and references to Appendices
BERTEAUCOURT-LES-DAMES. Billets. Aug 14ᵗʰ		Fine. P.S.R.
do. do. Billets. Aug 15ᵗʰ		Fine. P.S.R.
do. do. Billets. Aug 16ᵗʰ		Fine. P.S.R.
do. do. Billets. Aug 17		Fine. P.S.R.
do. do. Billets. Aug 18ᵗʰ	Little rain afternoon	P.S.R.
do. do. Billets. Aug 19ᵗʰ		Fine. P.S.R.
do. do. Billets. Aug 20ᵗʰ	Capᵗⁿ A.N. GAVIN-JONES and 4 Spears left on a Scout Tuition.	P.S.R. Fine.
do. do. do. Aug 21ˢᵗ Billets.	Yesterday evening received orders for the Brigade to occupy AUTHUILLE vide Appˣ A attached	P.S.R.

1915

WAR DIARY of 36th JACOB'S HORSE
or
INTELLIGENCE SUMMARY.

P. 53.
Army Form C. 2118.

(Erase heading not required.)

Hour, Date, Place	Summary of Events and Information	Remarks and references to Appendices
BERTEAUCOURT-LES-DAMES Aug. 22nd	L't R.D. OWEN-JONES & 26 other Ranks marched to 73rd H.d Qrs at 6.30 AM from whence they proceeded in Motor Lorries to VARF FORCEVILLE. The men were to bring back the horses of the Regiment. 2nd L't E.N. WALDRON, "A" Echelon with 2 G.S. Wagons & B Echelon with 21 other ranks (horse holders) marched to FORCEVILLE starting at 1.30 P.M. The Regiment (though 1st and water) marched at 3 P.M. to join the Brigade at the Rendez-vous at 4 P.M. at WARGNIES. L't Col: R.S. ROOME ..... in command of the Brigade Kirsch Party and in command at AUTHUILLE. Major E.A. FAGAN ..... In command of Regimental Kirsch Party Major W.G. GREEN ..... and 2nd in Comd " Capt. H.M. DAVIDSON ..... D. Sqdn —— " M.M. CARPENDALE ..... B " Lieut. the Hon. M. R.A. ADDINGTON ..A " 2/Lieut. C.L. REID ..... C " Lieut. M.F. PARNELL ..... Machine Guns " R.D. OWEN-JONES ..... Bombs	

P. 54
Army Form C. 2118.

WAR DIARY of 36th JACOB'S HORSE
or
INTELLIGENCE SUMMARY.
(Erase heading not required.)

1915

Instructions regarding War Diaries and Intelligence Summaries are contained in F.S. Regs., Part II. and the Staff Manual respectively. Title pages will be prepared in manuscript.

Hour, Date, Place	Summary of Events and Information	Remarks and references to Appendices
Aug 22nd Con 15	To bring back the horses. Capts Acpl. C.F. CAHUSAC. Capt. ROBINSON Capt. LORD KESTEVEN. Lincolnshire Yeomany. attd. Lt. ROBERTSON. Scotts Horse attd. "A" party Strength of Three. for AUTHUILE. 9 B.OS. 10 I.O.S. & 300 Sabres. "B" Strength of Above to ditto. 4 B.OS 6 I.O.S. & 94 Sabres. The above 2 parties left by route march. "A" party on arrival at 11 P.M at FORCEVILLE went into bivouac in the wood to the EAST of FORCEVILLE and remained there. Concealed till 5 P.M. 23rd inst. It was a cold wet night. Everyone much bitten by hornet bugs. "B" party remained at FORCEVILLE until 2 A.M 23rd inst when they	

P. 55

WAR DIARY of 36ᵃ JACOBS HORSE
or
INTELLIGENCE SUMMARY.

1915

Army Form C. 2118.

(Erase heading not required.)

Instructions regarding War Diaries and Intelligence Summaries are contained in F.S. Regs., Part II. and the Staff Manual respectively. Title pages will be prepared in manuscript.

Hour, Date, Place	Summary of Events and Information	Remarks and references to Appendices
FORCE	Followed the lead horses of the AMBALA B⁹ᵈᵉ back to BEAUCOURT arriving there at 5 AM 23ʳᵈ inst. They marched back to BERTEAUCOURT-LES-DAMES arriving there at 11 P.M.	"B" party was increased by the N⁰ 7 dismounted men who had gone in to bring out G.S. Waggons.
FORCEVILLE BIVOUAC 23ʳᵈ inst. 8. P.M.	"A" party assembled with the Brigade at 8 P.M. and marched on foot to MARTINSART (arriving 9 P.M.) where they met the guides told off to conduct them to AUTHUILE. Squadrons left MARTINSART at 3 minutes interval marching through AVELUY wood. The relief of SECUNDERABAD Bᵈᵉ was completed by 11 P.M. at AUTHUILE. The night passed without incident.	
11. P.M.		P.S.R.
AUTHUILE. 24ᵗʰ	The French Party was engaged in digging & working at the defences. No incidents.	
BERTEAUCOURT LES DAMES. 24ᵗʰ	Horses Exercised.	T.P.R.

P 56

Army Form C. 2118.

WAR DIARY of 36th JACOB'S HORSE 1915
or
INTELLIGENCE SUMMARY.
(Erase heading not required.)

Instructions regarding War Diaries and Intelligence Summaries are contained in F. S. Regs., Part II. and the Staff Manual respectively. Title pages will be prepared in manuscript.

Hour, Date, Place	Summary of Events and Information	Remarks and references to Appendices
AUTHUILE Aug. 25th	The French party engaged in digging & working at the defences - the working party came under machine gun fire to cause loss. 2nd Lieut R.F. ROOME handed over command of AUTHUILE & the trenches to our French Party to Lt Col SAUNDERS 24th Flanders & Hennuit to BERTEAUCOURT LES DAMES.	
BERTEAUCOURT LES DAMES Aug 25"	Billets. Horses Picketed. Fine.	PSB.
BERTEAUCOURT LES DAMES Aug 26" Aug 27" Aug 28" Aug 29"	Horses Exercised. Fine " " " Fine " " " Rain in afternoon Re-inforcements of 2 British Officers 1 Indian Officer and 99	
Aug 30"	Other ranks (dismounted) arrived Today	BSB
	The diary of the French Party at AUTHUILE will be entered in next Months diary when received.	RLQ

P. 57

Army Form C. 2118.

WAR DIARY of 36th Jacob's Horse
or
INTELLIGENCE SUMMARY.
(Erase heading not required.)

Instructions regarding War Diaries and Intelligence Summaries are contained in F.S. Regs., Part II. and the Staff Manual respectively. Title pages will be prepared in manuscript.

Hour, Date, Place	Summary of Events and Information	Remarks and references to Appendices
BERTEAUCOURT LES DAMES Aug 31st	Billets. Horse exercises. Fine.	C.T.
	(F. Ahuwal), Captain Adjutant for Commanding 36th Jacob's Horse 1st September 1915	

121/7286

Serial No 112.

WAR DIARY
OF
36th Jacob's Horse.

From 1st September 1915 To 30th September 1915

1915
WAR DIARY of the 36 JACOB'S HORSE P.58
or
INTELLIGENCE SUMMARY.   Army Form C. 2118.
(Erase heading not required.)

Hour, Date, Place	Summary of Events and Information	Remarks and references to Appendices

AUTHUILE
Aug. 26ᵗʰ

Diary continued of AUTHUILE Trench party from August 25ᵗʰ

Work continued on the perimeter of the village. 1 NCO & 14 men
A Sqdn at work 8 P.M. to midnight. Two or three shrapnel over front
near the village in the evening.

27ᵗʰ Working parties 7.30 – 11.30 A.M. 11.30 – 3.30 P.M. and 3.30 – 7.30 P.M.
A few shells near village before noon and a few after 8 P.M.

28ᵗʰ Working parties as yesterday. Few shells north end of village
during day.
10301 Sgt. ABDUL KARIM KHAN B/L killed wounded in leg. Evacuated

29ᵗʰ Working parties same as yesterday. Merry xxxx in evening
Night work (6 – 12 midnight) cancelled.
10 3055 S. CHANAN SINGH A Sqn killed by shell splinter whilst
head digging.

30ᵗʰ Working parties as yesterday.
1 NCO & 14 men told off to dig in turn for Brigade Signalling.

1915

WAR DIARY of 36th JACOB'S HORSE
or
INTELLIGENCE SUMMARY.

(Erase heading not required.)

Army Form C. 2118.
P 59

Hour, Date, Place	Summary of Events and Information	Remarks and references to Appendices
AUTHUILE (con'td) Aug 31st	Work as before. Rissaldar DARGAI KHAN 37th Lancers (att'd) killed 3.30 AM by a shell while on rounds visiting the piquet. No 2642 S. NUR MUHAMMAD KHAN wounded in foot by killed (slight) at 4 AM. Evacuated.	
Sept. 1st	Work as before but 1/2 2nd relief & whole 3rd relief knocked off. Heavy rain afternoon and night. 3 Officers 20th Deccan Horse arrived & take over on relief. No working parties. Packing & loading for departure on relief. Rain morning till 11 AM.	
" 2nd	Relief (20th Deccan Horse) arrived 12 midnight. Marched at 12.35 AM for FORCEVILLE WOOD to join led horses. Movements of Officers. Capt FARRAR on HAR returned from leave on 24th Sept Capt H M DAVIDSON & Lieut R.O. OWEN JONES returned on 26th by Capt LORD KESTEVEN & Lieut W. F. BLACKER.	

P. 60.

Army Form C. 2118.

1915

WAR DIARY of the 36 JACOB'S HORSE
or
INTELLIGENCE SUMMARY.
(Erase heading not required.)

Instructions regarding War Diaries and Intelligence
Summaries are contained in F.S. Regs., Part II.
and the Staff Manual respectively. Title pages
will be prepared in manuscript.

Hour, Date, Place	Summary of Events and Information	Remarks and references to Appendices
BERTEADCOURT-LES-DAMES. Sept. 2nd	The led horses for trench digging party left for FORCEVILLE WOOD at 3.P.M. Under command of Capt. C.F. CATHUSAC. Joining in with the led horses of the Brigade at WARGNIES at 4.P.M.	163 Officers' mounts. L.G.B. horses.
Sept. 3rd 2nd	Arrived at FORCEVILLE WOOD at 8.P.M. Trench party arrived at 3.AM & the Regiment marched to FRECHEN COURT.	
	The Regiment remained here to dig at SENLIS.	
	The following Officers returned to Head Quarters:— Major GREEN, Capt. CARPENDALE, Lieuts. PARNELL, BLACKER, Capt. LORD KESTEVEN, Lieut. ADDINGTON, 2nd Lieut. WALDRON, REID with 163 men.	
	Officers left with digging party. —	
	Major FAGAN, Capt. FARQUHAR, ROBINSON, Lieut. ROBERTSON, & HEARD & HARRISON.	
Sept. 4th	Billets cleaning up.	
Sept. 5th	Major FAGAN returned to H.Q. Gp.	
Sept. 6th 11.30.P.M.	Capt. DAVIDSON joined digging Party. Capt. FARQUHAR, Lieut. ROBERTSON & HARRISON & 170 men arrived from FRECHENCOURT, leaving me 3 Offrs & 132 other ranks.	+ Capt. DAVIDSON. " ROBINSON. Lieut. SHEARD

P. 61.

Army Form C. 2118.

1915

WAR DIARY of 36th JACOB'S HORSE
or
INTELLIGENCE SUMMARY.

(Erase heading not required.)

Hour, Date, Place	Summary of Events and Information	Remarks and references to Appendices
BERTEAUCOURT-LES-DAMES Sep. 7th	Billets.	Fine. R.S.R.
" Sep. 8th	14 men left for FRECHENCOURT for guard duties	Fine. R.S.R.
" Sep. 9th	Billets.	Fine. R.S.R.
" Sep. 10th	Billets.	Fine. R.S.R.
Sep. 11th	A party though all ranks marched at 7 P.M. to the trenches at AUTHUILE British Officers. Major E.A. FAGAN in command. Capt. C.F. CAMUSAC Adjutant. Capt. W.F.R. FARQUHAR C Sqn L.t M.E. PARNELL M Sqn. L.t W.F. BLACKER. D Sqn.	L.t R.D. OWEN-JONES. Bombs. L.t J. ROBERTSON (Scottish Horse) attd. 2nd Lt. HARISON (IARO) attd. Capt A.C. MUNRO. I.M.S.

WAR DIARY of 36th JACOB'S HORSE

or INTELLIGENCE SUMMARY

1915

Army Form C. 2118.

P 62

(Erase heading not required.)

Instructions regarding War Diaries and Intelligence Summaries are contained in F.S. Regs., Part II. and the Staff Manual respectively. Title pages will be prepared in manuscript.

Hour, Date, Place	Summary of Events and Information	Remarks and references to Appendices
Sep 11th Cou 15	10 Indian Officers. 280. Rifles. 20 M. guns. 16. Leading Pack mules. 2. G.S. Wagons 1. Mess Cart. 169 Horse letters accompanied the party. Leave train. The horses from the Trenches The truck party left for FRECHENCOURT al 7.P.M. The number too late to be completed by the inclusion of the men already digging at that place. The Brigade assembled at WARGNIES at 8 P.M. marching thence via TALMAS, and MOLLIENS-AU-BOIS. Arrived FRECHENCOURT 11:15 P.M. & spent the night there.	

1915
WAR DIARY of 36th JACOB'S HORSE
or
INTELLIGENCE SUMMARY
(Erase heading not required.)

Army Form C. 2118.
P 63

Hour, Date, Place	Summary of Events and Information	Remarks and references to Appendices
Sept 11th Egn (a)	Lieut I. ROBERTSON % Scottish Horse and 2 Jrs A.W. HARRISON & R.D. atta. left at 12 noon to take over horses from 30th Division Horse at AUTHUILE.	
Sept. 12th.	Truck party marched at 6.40 PM via MONTIGNY, BEAUCOURT, WARLOY and FORCEVILLE WOOD to MARTINSART. 2 g.s. wagons & medical accompanied the party. The figures and distributed at follows:— Truck Party (a) B.O. I.O. O.R. Transport. 6. 10. 293. 12. IORs. 1 Draughts 8 Draught. Horse Holders (b). 3. 4. 155. 5 " 10 horses. (a). Majr FAGAN, Capt FARQUHAR, CAHUSAC — Lieuts PARNELL BLACKER, OWEN JONES, joined by Lieuts ROBERTSON & HARRISON already in the trenches. (b). Capt R. DAVIDSON, Capt ROBINSON, Lieut SHEARS (2ILH) at MARTINSART. Truck Party dismounted (Ich—	T.E.R.

Army Form C. 2118.

P.64

WAR DIARY of 36th Jacob's Horse
or
INTELLIGENCE SUMMARY.
(Erase heading not required.)

Hour, Date, Place	Summary of Events and Information	Remarks and references to Appendices
Sept 12th Contd	Horses being marched back to fields, arriving there at 7 P.M. (13 hrs) and watered by squadrons at intervals of 3 minutes. to AUTHUILE, where it relieved 20th Deccan Horse & went into the same position as previously occupied. Relief completed by 12.45 A.M. 13 inst.	
Sept 13th AUTHUILE	Digging parties of 135 men each furnished from 10 A.M. to 2 P.M. and from 2 P.M. to 6 P.M. Working on fire and communication trenches in and around AUTHUILE. Slight shelling by enemy during digging both morning & evening. Capt. CARPENDALE arrived to take over command. 9 P.M. the Lord ROBERTSON returned to Reg'l H.Qrs.	

1915
WAR DIARY of 36th JACOB'S HORSE
or
INTELLIGENCE SUMMARY.

Army Form C. 2118.

P.65.

Hour, Date, Place	Summary of Events and Information	Remarks and references to Appendices
Sept 14th AUTHUILE	Digging party of 130 men from 7.30AM to 11AM working on the same trenches as yesterday. Marched at noon and took over the frontline trenches known as G.I. from the 30 Lancers - in the following order from the right D-B-C Sqn, A Sqn in support. Stood to arms from 7 to 8 P.M. light period generally. No enemy action. The parapet slightly damaged by shell fire.	
do Sept 15th	In the early hours of the morning (15th) two casualties occurred - 2671 Sow. AHMED KHAN C Sqn wounded 3293 " SHAHBAZ KHAN C " trunnel by parapet being in on him. Working parties during the day. 30 men from C & A Sqn repairing front trench & building a new fire trench. 50 men from B & A Sqn digging communication trench	RHB

Army Form C. 2118.

1915
WAR DIARY of 34~~Jacobs~~on
3D JACOB'S HORSE
or
INTELLIGENCE SUMMARY.
(Erase heading not required.)

p 66

Hour, Date, Place	Summary of Events and Information	Remarks and references to Appendices
15th Con. 6.	There was no unusual firing by the Enemy. Capt~~ain~~ LORD KESTEVEN, & ROBINSON killed to rejoin their Regiment, proceeding	The BATTERFLIES. RcB.
16th	During last night the machine corporal led the French hussars to a bombardment of a cellar opposite the hind on our right held by the 2d French Zouaves. Hot Rubato. Casualties during the night. 3097 Dafr. DURKHAN 35th Horse attacked. wounded slightly 2948 Gun. A-7TH ULLAH. 29th " " 3105 S. AHMED KHAN D. Sq my " " NZ men killed by 2 companies of the 7th Black Watch at 9.30.P.M. Squadrons marched back independently to FRESENVILLE Wood when they were met by the lead horse party under Major GREEN.	RcR
17th Ap~~ri~~l	The Regiment from there to FRECHEN COURT (L.M. 17.).	

1915

WAR DIARY of 36th JACOB'S HORSE

or

INTELLIGENCE SUMMARY.

(Erase heading not required.)

Army Form C. 2118.

P. 67

Hour, Date, Place	Summary of Events and Information	Remarks and references to Appendices
17th	Hackthorn left 6.30 P.M and marched to BERTEAUCOURT les DAMES arriving there 10 P.M.	RER
18th BERTEAUCOURT LES DAMES, Billets		Fine RER
do. 19th	Billets	Fine RER
do. 20th	Billets. 2nd in/c F.B. MALTBY) Spent morn, watching Fine RER. his arrival & was attached to the Machine Gun Section. #	
do. 21st	Divisional Field Day during which the Division was turned up for inspection by Field Marshall LORD KITCHENER. After the inspection the Regiment Marched to billets	Fine RER
22.	At 6.20am orders received to march to new billeting area. The Regiment being allotted LONGUEVILLETTE Ter	RER

Army Form C. 2118.

1915

WAR DIARY of 36th Jacob's HORSE
or
INTELLIGENCE SUMMARY.

(Erase heading not required.)

Instructions regarding War Diaries and Intelligence Summaries are contained in F.S. Regs., Part II. and the Staff Manual respectively. Title pages will be prepared in manuscript.

p. 68

Hour, Date, Place	Summary of Events and Information	Remarks and references to Appendices
LONGUEVILLETTE 22nd Sept.	The Regiment marched at 12.30 P.M. and arrived at LONGUEVILLETTE at 3.15 P.M. Fine	PCR
do. do. 23rd Sept.	Horses very scarce in village. Horses had to go to HEM (3 miles) to be watered. Drills in relays. 100 Neps. 2 pounds each. Filthy water in billets of horses. Strong with sulphurilled - hydrogen. Began to rain heavily in the evening.	PCR
do. do. 24th Sept.	Rained all last night & practically all day. Received orders to be ready to move at 2½ Hours notice.	PCR
do. do. 25 Sept	Rained all last night. Copy of a memo no C-1824 d/17 Sept. 1915 from Genl. Maffé Indian Car Corps. "The Army Commander would be glad if you would express to all ranks of the Indian Cavalry Car Corps his appreciation of the work they have done in the trenches. The holding of a portion of the line by the Indian Cavalry Corps and the support given by the R.H.A. batteries has been of great assistance to the Army, and although companies were new to the conditions of trench warfare, all ranks of the Indian Cavalry Corps have carried out their duties in accordance with the best traditions of the British Army."	PCR

1915

WAR DIARY of 36TH JACOB'S HORSE
or
INTELLIGENCE SUMMARY.

(Erase heading not required.)

Army Form C. 2118.

P. 69

Instructions regarding War Diaries and Intelligence Summaries are contained in F.S. Regs., Part II. and the Staff Manual respectively. Title pages will be prepared in manuscript.

Hour, Date, Place	Summary of Events and Information	Remarks and references to Appendices
LONGUEVILLETTE. Sept. 25th Tou/a	At received orders to be at one hour's notice from time of receipt at Bde H.Q.'s. To saddle up & be ready to start at once. At 5 P.M. Rations were drawn. At 9.45 P.M. received orders that we might immediately to remain in a state of instant readiness. Also 10 P.M. received orders that the Regiment would not be required to move till 5 P.M. After 5 P.M. to be in a state of two minutes readiness.	P.S. Arrangements for carrying 2 days emergency rations on pack transport completed. 2 days iron rations on Bridget. R.P. Rawalal night. R.P.
Sept. 26th do	5 A.M. Regiment in a state of two minutes readiness. 4.30 P.M. Regiment placed in a state of 2½ hours readiness. Demolition party organised (L.P., 2 N.C.O's & 6 men)	Fine, dull day. R.P.
Sept. 27th do	Rained during the night. Regimental Intelligence Arrangements re-organised (W.O.T. Price & N.C.O. Brown from Sect. Sqd.)	R.P.
Sept. 28th do	Reich:	Rain. R.P.
Sept. 29th do	Birth:	Heavy rain during the day. R.P.
Sept. 30th do	Birth:	Fine. R.P.

R.G. Tague Hat Comd. 36/Jacob's Horse, 3/9/15.

Serial No. 112.

Confidential

121/7601

War Diary

of

36th Jacob's Horse.

FROM 1st October 1915. TO 31st October 1915.

1915.

WAR DIARY of 36th JACOB'S HORSE Army Form C. 2118.

or INTELLIGENCE SUMMARY

P. 70.

(Erase heading not required.)

Instructions regarding War Diaries and Intelligence Summaries are contained in F. S. Regs., Part II. and the Staff Manual respectively. Title pages will be prepared in manuscript.

Hour, Date, Place	Summary of Events and Information	Remarks and references to Appendices
LONGUEVILLETTE Oct. 1st	Divisional Scheme.	Fine. RSR.
do Oct. 2nd	Reco at SANT SING HL (93rd) Carried out Reconnoitred this posn until trisetalunes	Fine. R.S.R.
do Oct. 3rd	B.U.b. Parade. At 4.30 PM received orders to be at 4 hours notice	Fine. ReR.
do Oct. 4th	Brigade Parade.	Showery intervals of sunshine. R.S.R.
do Oct. 5th	Divisional Exercise.	Rain x wind. ReR.
do Oct. 6th	B.U.b.	Fine. R.R.
Oct. 7th do	Brigade Staff tour.	Fine R.S.R

1915

WAR DIARY of 6th JACOBS HORSE

or

INTELLIGENCE SUMMARY.

(Erase heading not required.)

Army Form C. 2118.

P. 71

Hour, Date, Place	Summary of Events and Information	Remarks and references to Appendices
LONGUEVILLETTE. Oct 8th.	Divisional Exercise. Fine	R.C.B.
do. Oct. 9th.	Brig's. Inspection by G.O.C. Brigade of turnout, kit, men mounted. Fine. Ahorsed & infantry men do, receiving leave July 1st 1915.	R.C.B.
Oct. 10th. do.	Inspection of kits & horses by G.O.C. B'de. Fine. At 3. P.M. received orders that we were to be at 10 hours notice.	R.C.B.
Oct. 11th. do.	Brigade Scheme. Fine.	R.C.B.
Oct. 12th. do.	Drills. Fine.	R.C.B.
Oct. 13th.	Changed billets to BERNAVILLE at 2 P.M. Fine.	R.C.B.
Oct. 14th. BERNAVILLE.	Drills. Misty - Fine.	R.C.B.

1915
WAR DIARY of 6th JACOB'S HORSE.
or
INTELLIGENCE SUMMARY.

Army Form C. 2118.

P. 72

Hour, Date, Place	Summary of Events and Information	Remarks and references to Appendices
BERNAVILLE. Oct. 15.	Divisional Exercise. 16 Pack Cobs received. This completes the Machine Gun section which are all (4) carried on pack. Very dense mist.	ReR
do. Oct. 16th	Billets.	True ReR.
Oct. 17th do	Billets. Weather - mist very light and variable mainly from South and East - dull & windy.	ReR.
Oct. 18th do.	Corps Scheme. Mist light and variable at first becoming South Easterly later - Weather dull and hazy at first becoming clearer finally.	ReR.

1915

WAR DIARY
or
INTELLIGENCE SUMMARY.

38th Jacob's Horse Army Form C. 2118.

P 73.

(Erase heading not required.)

Hour, Date, Place	Summary of Events and Information	Remarks and references to Appendices
BERNAVILLE. October 19th.	Billets.	Purely at rest. Weather fine. R&R.
do. October 20th.	Inspection of M. Guns by C.O. & B.M. Two Vickers guns relined - thus completing 4 Vickers guns with the Regiment	Probably at rest. Weather fine. R&R.
October 21st do	Received orders last night to move into a new area. Rained heavily at 10.P.M	R&R.
October 22nd OISSY. RIENCOURT & LE MESGE.	The Brigade marched into its new billeting area. The Regiment was billeted as under:- H.Q. & "C" Sqdn at OISSY. "A" & "D" Sqdns at RIENCOURT. "B" & M. GUNS at LE MESGE. Weather fine.	R&R.

Army Form C. 2118.

P.74.

WAR DIARY of 36th JACOB'S HORSE.
or
INTELLIGENCE SUMMARY.
(Erase heading not required.)

Instructions regarding War Diaries and Intelligence Summaries are contained in F.S. Regs., Part II. and the Staff Manual respectively. Title pages will be prepared in manuscript.

Hour, Date, Place	Summary of Events and Information	Remarks and references to Appendices
DISSY, RIENCOURT & LEMESCE. Oct 23rd	Orders have been received that representatives of Cavalry units of the Indian Cavalry Corps will parade to be inspected by H.M. THE KING. Each Regiment will be represented by one squadron composed of one troop from each squadron of the Regiment with a corresponding proportion of officers. ETAT DE TRUPE. Com. A Composite Regt. formed of the 3 Composite Squadrons of the Brigade. Lieut. Oglas Jones acting as Adjutant. Major Facon - Com. of Sqn. Captn. Davison 2nd in Com. of Sqn.	True
do. Oct 24th	Parade above countermanded. 2 Lieut. W. CHUBB reported his arrival and posted to A Sqn. as	

WAR DIARY of 36th JACOBS HORSE / 1915.

Army Form C. 2118.
P.75.

Hour, Date, Place.	Summary of Events and Information.	Remarks and references to Appendices.
DISSY. RIENCOURT & LEMESSE Oct. 25th.	Billets. Heavy Rain all day.	R.R.
do. Oct. 26th.	Billets. Rain.	R.R.
do. Oct. 27th.	Billets. Lieut. C.L. REID I.A.R.O. transferred to do. Lieut. I. ROBERTSON transferred to his own Regt (18th Lancers). Fine.	R.R.
do Oct. 28th.	Billets. Indian Cavalry Corps ordered to parade for inspection by H.M. THE KING tomorrow. Anticipatory route march.	R.R.
do Oct. 29th F	Inspection postponed. Fine.	R.R.
do. Oct. 30th F.	Billets. Fine.	R.R.
do. Oct. 31st Sun	Billets. Rain.	R.R.

R.J. Roome Lt Col.
Comdg. 36th Jacob's Horse

1/11/15.

Serial No. 112.   12/780

Confidential

War Diary

of

36th Jacob's Horse.

FROM 1st November 1915 TO 30th November 1915

SERIAL NO. 112.

121/7780.

CONFIDENTIAL

WAR DIARY

OF

36TH JACOB'S HORSE.

FROM 1st November, 1915.

TO 30th November, 1915.

P.76.

Place.	Date.		Summary of Events and Information.		Remarks and references to Appendices.
OISSY, RIENCOURT & LEMESGES.	Nov. 1st	Billets		Rain	R.E.R.
	Nov. 2nd	Billets		Rain	R.E.R.
"	Nov. 3rd	Billets		Fine	R.E.R.
"	Nov. 4th	Billets	Major E.A. Fagan left to-day to take over Command 1/8 Liverpool Battn.	Rainy	R.E.R.
"	Nov. 5th	Billets		Fine	R.E.R.
"	Nov. 6th	Billets		Fine	R.E.R.
"	Nov. 7th	Billets		Fine Frost at night.	R.E.R.
"	Nov. 8th		The 1st Md. Cav. Divn. paraded to-day for the distribution of decorations presented by the French Government. R.No.2723 Dafedar Saiyid Hassain B. Sqdn. was presented with the Croix de Guerre for gallantry in action at FESTUBERT in January of this year. Captn. H.M. Davidson and Captn. A.N. Gavin-Jones left to-day to report to the War Office being appointed to Infantry Battalions.	Fine	
"	Nov. 9th	Billets		Fine	R.E.R.
"	Nov.10th	Billets		Rainy	R.E.R.

Place.	Date	Summary of Events and Information.	Remarks and references to Appendices.
OISSY, RIENCOURT & LEMESGE.	Nov. 11th	The Indian Cavalry Corps paraded for inspection by Genl. Sir E.H. Allenby, K.C.B. Comdg. III Army. The II Indian Cavy. Divn. were presented with French Decorations. The Corps marched past by Squadrons. Present on parade 76 Squadrons, 6 Batt. R.H.A., 18 Machine Gun Detachments (72 Guns). Strong cold wind, rain squalls.	R.E.R.
"	Nov. 12th	Billets Rain.	
"	Nov. 13th	Billets 2nd Lt. P.P. Braithwaite I.A.R.O. 2nd Lt. H.R. Landale I.A.R.O. reported their arrival to join the Regiment. Rain.	R.E.R.
"	Nov. 14th	Billets Rained in morning. Fine afternoon.	R.E.R.
"	Nov. 15th	Billets. Snow fell this morning	R.E.R.
"	Nov. 16th	Billets. Snowed heavily in the morning, fine afterwards.	R.E.R.
"	Nov. 17th	Billets. Partial thaw, still cold.	R.E.R.
FONTAINE, WANEL & SOREL.	Nov. 18th	Moved into a new billeting area To-day. Regiment distributed as under:— at FONTAINE Hd. Qrs. "B" Sqdn. and Dismounted men (temporarily) " WANEL "A" and "C" Sqdns. " SOREL "D" Sqdn. and Machine Guns. Thawing slightly at times still very cold.	R.E.R.

Place.	Date.	Summary of Events and Information.	Remarks and references to Appendices.
FONTAINE, WANEL & SOREL	Nov. 19th Billets.	Gradual thaw continued.	W.G.
	Nov. 20th Billets.	Gradual thaw continued.	W.G.
"	Nov. 21st Billets.	Lt.Col. R.E. Roome departed on Sick leave Maj. W.G.K. Green assumed temporary command. Thaw continued.	W.G.
"	Nov. 22nd Billets	Dry.	W.G.
"	Nov. 23rd Billets	Dry - Slight Frost.	W.G.
"	Nov. 24th Billets	Dry - Slight Frost.	W.G.
"	Nov. 25th Billets	Captn. J.N. Simonds, 35th S.H., Joined from England, for duty. Bright Sunshine - Cold.	W.G.
"	Nov. 26th Billets	Bright Sunshine, morning. Frost.	W.G.
"	Nov. 27th Billets	Hard Frost.	W.G.
"	Nov. 28th Billets	Hard Frost.	W.G.
"	Nov. 29th Billets	Lieut. R.D. Owen Jones, 1 Ind. Offr. and 4 N.C.O's commenced a 10 days course of instruction in Trench Warfare, with 1st Ind. Fd. Sqn. LIOMER. Rain from early morning and all day.	W.G.
"	Nov. 30th Billets.	Bright sunshine all day. Heavy rain at night.	W.G.

(Sgd.) W.G.K. Green Major
Comdg. 36th Jacob's Horse.

Army Form C. 2118.

P 76

WAR DIARY

B 26/Jacob's HORSE.

or

INTELLIGENCE SUMMARY.

1915

(Erase heading not required.)

Hour, Date, Place.		Summary of Events and Information.	Remarks and references to Appendices.
DISSY. RIENCOURT & LEMESGES. Nov. 1.	Billets.	Rain	ReP.
do Nov. 2nd	Billets	Rain.	ReP.
do Nov. 3rd	Billets	Fine	ReP.
do Nov. 4*	Billets. Major E.A. FAGAN left 16 day to take over command 1/8 Liverpool Regt.		ReP
do Nov. 5"	Billets.	Fine.	ReP
do Nov. 6"	Billets.	Fine	ReP,
do Nov 7	Billets.	Fine. Fine/slight	ReP.

WAR DIARY or INTELLIGENCE SUMMARY.

36th JACOB'S HORSE.

1915

Army Form C. 2118.
P. 77.

(Erase heading not required.)

Hour, Date, Place.	Summary of Events and Information.	Remarks and references to Appendices.
OISSY, RIENCOURT & LEMESGE. Nov. 8.	The 1st Ind. Cav. Div. paraded today for the distribution of decorations presented by the French Government. R. N° 2723 Lefetas Vaijid Hussain 13 Sqn was presented with the Croix de Guerre for gallantry in action at FESTUBERT in January of this year. Capt H.M. DAVIDSON & Capt A.N. GAVIN-JONES left to day to report to the War Office to his newly battalions.	Fine. R&R
do. Nov. 9th	Billets.	Fine. P.&R.
do. Nov. 10th	Billets.	Raining. R&R.

Army Form C. 2118.
P.78

WAR DIARY
or
INTELLIGENCE SUMMARY.

Of 36th JACOB'S HORSE.

1915

(Erase heading not required.)

Instructions regarding War Diaries and Intelligence Summaries are contained in F. S. Regs., Part II, and the Staff Manual respectively. Title pages will be prepared in manuscript.

Hour, Date, Place.	Summary of Events and Information.	Remarks and references to Appendices.
OISSY, RIENCOURT & LEMESGE. NOV. 11th	The Indian Cavalry Corps paraded for inspection by Genl. Sir. E.H.ALLENBY. K.C.B. Com'dg III Army. The II Indian Cav'y Div'n were presented with French Decorations. The Corps marched past by Brigades. Present on parade 76 Squadrons 6 Ba.H R.H.A, 13 Machine Gun Detachments (7 Pers). Strength during this Epistle.	R/R
do. NOV. 12th	Billets.	Rain. R/R
do. NOV. 13th	Billets. 2nd Lt. T.P.BRAITHWAITE I.A.R.O. 2nd Lt. H.R.LANDALE I.A.R.O. reported their arrival to join the Regiment.	Rain. R/R
do NOV. 14th	Billets.	Rain is turning fine afternoon. R/R

Gulab Singh & Sons, Calcutta—No. 22 Army C.—6-8-14—1,07,000.

Army Form C. 2118.

P 79

WAR DIARY or **INTELLIGENCE SUMMARY**

Of 35th Jacobs Horse

1915

(Erase heading not required.)

Hour, Date, Place.	Summary of Events and Information.	Remarks and references to Appendices.
DISSY, RIENCOURT & LEMESGE. Nov. 15th	Billets. Photos test this morning.	P.S.O.
do. Nov. 16th	Billets. Snowed heavily in the morning. Fine after wards.	P.S.O.
do. Nov. 17th	Billets. Partial thaw, still cold.	P.S.R.
Nov. 18th FONTAINE, WANEL & SOREL.	March. Moved into a new billeting area today. Regiment did billet as under:— a) FONTAINE — H.Qrs. "B" Sqn. & dismounted men (temporarily) WANEL — A & C. Sqns and SOREL — D Sqn. & Machine Guns. Thawing slightly at times, still very cold.	P.S.R.
do. Nov. 19th	Billets. Gradual thaw continued.	nil.

Army Form C. 2118.

p. 80.

WAR DIARY
or
INTELLIGENCE SUMMARY

1915 36th Jacob's Horse

(Erase heading not required.)

Instructions regarding War Diaries and Intelligence Summaries are contained in F. S. Regs., Part II, and the Staff Manual respectively. Title pages will be prepared in manuscript.

Hour, Date, Place.	Summary of Events and Information.	Remarks and references to Appendices.
FONTAINE, SOREL & WANEL. Nov. 20.	Billets. Gradual thaw continued.	JP.
do Nov. 21.	Billets. Lt.Col. R.E. Roome departed on sick leave (Maj. H.G.K. Green assumed temporary command) Thaw continued.	JP.
do Nov. 22.	Billets. Dry.	JP.
do Nov. 23.	Billets. Dry - Slight Frost.	JP.
do Nov. 24.	Billets. Dry - Slight Frost.	JP.
do Nov. 25.	Billets. Capt. J.N. Simonds, 35th S.H. joined from England, for duty. Bright sunshine - cold.	JP.
do Nov. 26.	Billets. Bright sunshine, morning. Frost.	JP.

Gulab Singh & Sons, Calcutta—No. 22 Army C.—5-8-14—1,07,000.

Army Form C. 2118.

WAR DIARY
or
INTELLIGENCE SUMMARY.

of 36th Jacob's Horse.

p. 81.

1915

(Erase heading not required.)

Instructions regarding War Diaries and Intelligence Summaries are contained in F. S. Regs., Part II, and the Staff Manual respectively. Title pages will be prepared in manuscript.

Hour, Date, Place.		Summary of Events and Information.	Remarks and references to Appendices.
FONTAINE, SOREL & WANEL Nov. 27.	Billets.	Hard Frost.	nil.
do Nov. 28.	Billets.	Hard Frost.	nil.
do Nov. 29.	Billets.	Lieut. R.S. Owen Jones, 1 Ind. Off: & 4 N.C.O.s commenced a 10 days course of instruction in Trench Warfare, with 1st Ind. 2nd Sqn. 21 OMER. Rain from early morning all day.	nil.
do Nov. 30.	Billets.	Bright Sunshine all day. Heavy rain at night.	nil.

W.J. Greenberger
Comdg. 36th Jacob's Horse.

Confidential

To

The D.A.G., G.H.Q. 3ᵈ Echelon
Army Head Quarters in India.

No J·H·948   dy 1.12.15

The War Diary for the month of November 1915 is forwarded herewith

　　　　　　　　　　　　　　　[signed] Major
Commanding 36ᵗʰ Jacobs Horse

Army Form C. 2118.

WAR DIARY of 36th Jacob's Horse
or
INTELLIGENCE SUMMARY.— 1 DIV Lucknow Cav Bde 7h

(Erase heading not required.)

1915

Instructions regarding War Diaries and Intelligence Summaries are contained in F. S. Regs., Part II, and the Staff Manual respectively. Title pages will be prepared in manuscript.

Hour, Date, Place.	Summary of Events and Information.	Remarks and references to Appendices.
DIGBY, RIENCOURT & LEMESGES. Nov. 1.	Billets.	None
do Nov. 2nd	Billets.	R.R.
do Nov. 3rd	Billets.	Rain. R.R.
do	Billets.	Fine R.R.
do Nov. 4th	Major E.A. FAGAN left today to take over command 1/B Unionist Rajput R.R.	R.R.
do Nov. 5	Billets.	Fine R.R.
do Nov. 6	Billets.	Fine R.R.
do Nov. 7	Billets.	Fine then later R.R.

Gulab Singh & Sons, Calcutta—No. 22 Army C.—5-8-14—1,07,000.

Army Form C. 2118.

WAR DIARY
or
INTELLIGENCE SUMMARY.

J 3B 1st TAIWE'S HORSE.   P. 77.

1915

(Erase heading not required.)

Hour, Date, Place.	Summary of Events and Information.	Remarks and references to Appendices.
OISSY, RIENCOURT & LEMESGE. Nov. 8.	The 1st Ind. Cav. Div. paraded today for the distribution of decorations presented by the French Government. R. No 2723 Lafadar Saujit Hassain 10 Sq. was presented with the Croix de Guerre for gallantry in action at FESTUBERT in January of this year. Capt H.M.DAVIDSON & Cap. A.H. GAVIN-JONES ypd. to-day to report the two officer being appointed to Infantry Battalions.	Fine. R&R
No. 1 Nov. 9.	March.	Fine. T&R
do Nov. 10.	Rested.	Raining. R&R

Army Form C. 2118.

P.78.

WAR DIARY
or
INTELLIGENCE SUMMARY.

Fj 3t JACOB'S HORSE.

1915

(Erase heading not required.)

Instructions regarding War Diaries and Intelligence Summaries are contained in F. S. Regs., Part II, and the Staff Manual respectively. Title pages will be prepared in manuscript.

Hour, Date, Place.	Summary of Events and Information.	Remarks and references to Appendices.
OISSY, RIENCOURT & LEMESGE. Nov. 11th	The Indian Cavalry Corps paraded for inspection by Genl. Sir E.H. ALLENBY. K.C.B. from 4th III Army. The II Indian Cav. Div. were presented with French decorations. The Corps marched past by Squadrons. Paraded on parade 76 Squadrons, 6 Batt RHA, 13 Machine Gun detachments (72 Guns), Infantry, Pioneers Transport etc.	R.R.
do. Nov. 12.	Billets. Rain.	R.R.
do. Nov. 13.	Billets. 2/Lt. T.P. BRAITHWAITE I.A.R.O. 2/Lt. H.R. LANDALE I.A.R.O. reported their arrival & joined the Regiment. Rain.	R.R.
do. Nov. 14th	Billets. Issued to every Front officer.	R.R.B.

Army Form C. 2118.

P 79.

WAR DIARY
or
INTELLIGENCE SUMMARY.

8 36th/Jacobs Horse

1915

(Erase heading not required.)

Hour, Date, Place.	Summary of Events and Information.	Remarks and references to Appendices.
OISSY, RIENCOURT & LEMESSE. Nov. 15th	Billets. Snow fell this morning.	P.S.B
do. Nov. 16th	Billets - Snowed heavily in the morning, fine afterwards.	P.S.B.
do. Nov. 17th	Billets - Partial thaw, still cold.	P.S.R.
do. Nov. 18th FONTAINE, WAMEL & SOREL.	Moved into a new billeting area today - Regiment distributed as under. (a) FONTAINE - H.Qrs. B Sqn & Hammerschmitt's team (temporarily) WAMEL - A & C Sqns. SOREL - D Sqn & Machine Guns. Thawing slightly at times still very cold.	P.S.R.
do Nov. 19th	Billets - Gradual thaw continued.	off.

Army Form C. 2118.

p. 80.

WAR DIARY or INTELLIGENCE SUMMARY.

1915 of 36th Jacob's Horse

(Erase heading not required.)

Instructions regarding War Diaries and Intelligence Summaries are contained in F. S. Regs., Part II, and the Staff Manual respectively. Title pages will be prepared in manuscript.

Hour, Date, Place.	Summary of Events and Information.	Remarks and references to Appendices.
FONTAINE, SOREL & WANEL. Nov. 20.	Billets. Gradual thaw continued.	nil.
do. Nov. 21.	Billets. Lt. Col. R. E. Roome departed on sick leave. Maj. N.G.K. Green assumed temporary command. Thaw continued.	nil.
do. Nov. 22.	Billets. Dry.	nil.
do. Nov. 23.	Billets. Dry - Slight frost.	nil.
do. Nov. 24.	Billets. Dry - Slight frost.	nil.
do. Nov. 25.	Billets. Capt. J.N. Simonds, 35th S.H., joined from England, for duty. Bright sunshine - cold.	nil.
do. Nov. 26.	Billets. Bright sunshine, morning. Frost.	nil.

Army Form C. 2118.

WAR DIARY

or

INTELLIGENCE SUMMARY.

1915 of 36th Jacob's Horse.

p. 81.

(Erase heading not required.)

Hour, Date, Place.		Summary of Events and Information.	Remarks and references to Appendices.
FONTAINE, SOREL & WANEL Nov. 27.	Billets.	Hard Frost.	nil.
do. Nov. 28.	Billets.	Hard Frost.	nil.
do Nov. 29.	Billets.	Lieut. R.B. Owen Jones, 1 Ind. Offr. & 4 N.C.O.s commenced a 10 days' course of instruction in Trench Warfare, with 1st Ind. 7.d. Sqn. LIOMER. Rain from early morning + all day.	nil.
do Nov. 30.	Billets.	Bright sunshine all day. Heavy rain at night.	nil.

[signature]
Comdg. 36th Jacob's Horse.

Lucknow

Serial No. 112.

Confidential
Weekly Diary
of
36th Jacob's Horse.

FROM 1st December 1915 TO 31st December 1915

Army Form C. 2118.

p. 82

WAR DIARY
1915 — of 36th Jacob's Horse
INTELLIGENCE SUMMARY.
(Erase heading not required.)

Instructions regarding War Diaries and Intelligence Summaries are contained in F. S. Regs., Part II, and the Staff Manual respectively. Title pages will be prepared in manuscript.

Hour, Date, Place.		Summary of Events and Information.	Remarks and references to Appendices.
FONTAINE, SOREL & NANEL.	Dec. 1.	Billets.	Morning fine. Rain at night. 2nd Lt. E.F. Ogley, I.A.R. joined to date with Regiment	J.B.
do	Dec. 2.	Billets.	Rain early morning + again at night from 5 p.m.	J.B.
do	Dec. 3.	Billets.	Rain continued till noon. Rain at intervals afternoon.	J.B.
do	Dec. 4.	Billets.	Slight rain all morning.	J.B.
do	Dec. 5.	Billets.	Morning fine. Heavy Rain afternoon.	J.B.
do	Dec. 6.	Billets.	Showers throughout the day.	J.B.
do	Dec. 7.	Billets.	The Regiment was inspected in Marching Order, + Squadrons at Sqn. Drill + M.G. Detachment in action, by the Corps Commander. Bright sunshine morning + forenoon; Rain afternoon.	
do	Dec. 8.	Billets.	Rain morning, to 11 a.m. Fine afternoon.	J.B.
do	Dec. 9.	Billets.	Rain from early morning + throughout the day.	J.B.
do	Dec. 10.	Billets.	Rain, morning till noon - + again at night.	J.B.
do	Dec. 11	Billets.	Heavy rain, morning.	J.B.
do	Dec. 12	Billets.	Slight frost at night.	J.B.
do	Dec. 13	Billets.	Frosty. Sunshine. Hard frost at night.	J.B.
do	Dec. 14	Billets.	Frost, morning. Wind changed to S.W. 10 a.m. Cloudy. Capt. M. M. Caspard(all ranks) rejoins from 1 months attachment to British Infantry for instruction in Trench Warfare	J.B.

Army Form C. 2118.

P. 83

WAR DIARY of 36th Jacob's Horse.
INTELLIGENCE SUMMARY.

(Erase heading not required.)

Instructions regarding War Diaries and Intelligence Summaries are contained in F. S. Regs., Part II, and the Staff Manual respectively. Title pages will be prepared in manuscript.

Hour, Date, Place.		Summary of Events and Information.	Remarks and references to Appendices.
FONTAINE, SOREL & WANEL	Dec. 15.	Billets. Dull. Cold. E. Wind. Rain afternoon.	nap.
FRANLEU CAMPAGNE HYMMEVILLE FRIREULLES	Dec. 16	Moved W.N.W. to new billeting area today. Regiment disposed as follows:— FRANLEU — Ht Qrs, C + D Sqn. and M.G. detacht CAMPAGNE — A Sqn. HYMMEVILLE — Officers of A Sqn — Dismounted men — Transport. FRIREULLES — B Sqn.	
		Weather: dull, cold, no rain.	
do	Dec. 17	Billets. Slight rain all day.	nap.
do	Dec. 18	do. Cold - No rain.	nap.
do	Dec. 19	do. Sunshine all morning.	nap.
do	Dec. 20	do. morning bright. aftern: dull.	nap.
do	Dec. 21	do Rain from early morning.	nap.
do	Dec. 22	do Rain from mid-day.	nap.
do	Dec. 23	do Rain.	nap.

Army Form C. 2118.

P. 84

WAR DIARY

of 36th Jacob's Horse.

1915

INTELLIGENCE SUMMARY.

(Erase heading not required.)

Instructions regarding War Diaries and Intelligence Summaries are contained in F. S. Regs., Part II, and the Staff Manual respectively. Title pages will be prepared in manuscript.

Hour, Date, Place.			Summary of Events and Information.	Remarks and references to Appendices.
FRANLEU CAMPAGNE HYMMEVILLE FRIREULLES	Dec. 24.	Billets.	Rain.	nil.
do	Dec 25	do.	Fine.	nil.
do	Dec 26	do.	Sunshine.	nil.
do	Dec 27	do.	do.	nil.
do	Dec 28	do.	do.	nil.
do	Dec 29	do.	Rain in afternoon.	nil.
do	Dec 30	do.	Fine.	nil.
do	Dec 31	do.	Dull — no rain morning — slight rain afternoon.	nil.

W. Skeen Major
Comdg 36th Jacob's Horse.

1/1/16

SERIAL NO. 112.

Confidential

War Diary

of

21st Jacob's Horse.

FROM 1st January 1916 TO 31st January 1916.

Army Form C. 2118.

p. 85

WAR DIARY of 36th Jacob's Horse

INTELLIGENCE SUMMARY. 1916.

(Erase heading not required.)

Hour, Date, Place.			Summary of Events and Information.	Remarks and references to Appendices.
FRANLEU CAMPAGNE HYMMEVILLE FRIREULLES	Jan. 1	Billets.	Stormy; some rain. Divisional Inter-Regimental Marathon Race, 6 miles. 240 Starters; No 2819 L.D. Harnam Singh ran second.	AB.
do	Jan. 2	do.	Rain morning.	AB.
do	Jan. 3	do.	Some rain at intervals.	AB.
do	Jan. 4	do.	do.	AB.
do	Jan. 5	do.	Sunshine all morning & latter part of afternoon. Lieut. R.D. OWEN JONES accidentally killed through premature explosion of a hand grenade.	AB.
do	Jan. 6	do.	Rain at intervals throughout the day	AB.
do	Jan. 7	do.	Inspection of Brigade in marching-order by G.O.C., 1st Indian Cavalry Division. Morning fine, afternoon wet.	AB.
do	Jan. 8	do.	Funeral of Lieut. R.D. Owen Jones at ABBEVILLE. Weather fine till 6 P.M. Rain evening & night. Capt. J. GRAVES, I.V., attached, joined the Regt.	AB.
do	Jan. 9	do.	Fine.	AB.
do	Jan. 10	do.	Slight rain.	AB.
do	Jan. 11	do.		AB.

Army Form C. 2118.

p. 86.

WAR DIARY
of 36th Jacob's Horse.
1916
INTELLIGENCE SUMMARY.

Instructions regarding War Diaries and Intelligence Summaries are contained in F. S. Regs., Part II, and the Staff Manual respectively. Title pages will be prepared in manuscript.

(Erase heading not required.)

Hour, Date, Place.		Summary of Events and Information.	Remarks and references to Appendices.
FRANLEU CAMPAGNE HYMEVILLE FRIREULLES	Jan: 12. Billets	Morning fine - Heavy rain, evening.	nil.
	Jan: 13. do.	Dull, stormy.	nil.
	Jan: 14. do.	Fine. Sunshine all morning.	nil.
	Jan: 15. do.	Rain early morning.	nil.
	Jan: 16. do.	Dull.	nil.
	Jan: 17. do.	Slight frost early morning. Rain afternoon.	nil.
	Jan: 18. do.	Dull, some rain.	nil.
	Jan: 19. do.	Sunshine.	nil.
	Jan: 20. do.	J. H. Dismounted Squadron inspected by G.O.C. Brigade, on a Route March.	nil.
	Jan: 21. do.	} Weather dull - Drizzle occasionally.	nil.
	Jan: 22. do.		nil.
	Jan: 23. do.		nil.
	Jan: 24. do.		nil.
	Jan: 25. do.	Bright sunshine all day. Slight frost early morning.	nil.
	Jan: 26. do.	Slight rain, morning.	nil.
	Jan: 27. do.	Dull morning - slight rain, evening.	nil.

Army Form C. 2118.

p. 87.

WAR DIARY

~~INTELLIGENCE SUMMARY.~~

of 30th Jacob's Horse.

1916.

(*Erase heading not required.*)

Hour, Date, Place.		Summary of Events and Information.	Remarks and references to Appendices.
FRANLEU CAMPAGNE HYMMEVILLE FRIREULLES	Jan: 28. Billets.	J.H. Dismounted Squadron inspected, in a trench assault by G.O.C. Brigade.	sgd.
	" 29 Billets.		sgd.
	" 30 Billets.	misty morning - slight single evening.	sgd.
	" 31 Billets.		sgd.

Wyndham Major
Comdg. 36th Jacob's Horse.

SERIAL NO. 112

Confidential
War Diary
of
36th Jacob's Horse

FROM 1st February 1916 TO 29th February 1916

Army Form C. 2118.

WAR DIARY of 36th Jacob's Horse

1916.

INTELLIGENCE SUMMARY.

(Erase heading not required.)

p. 88.

Hour, Date, Place.		Summary of Events and Information.	Remarks and references to Appendices.
FRANLEU CAMPAGNE HYMMEVILLE FRIEULLES	Feb: 1	Billets. Dry. Cold kind.	On 30th January :- 1 J.O. + 56 men made comm. of 2nd Lieut. A.W. Harrison (I.A.R.) proceeded to 7th Corps for employment on defence works. qp
"	2	do. Temp. 2nd Lieut. R.G. Faithfull attached. Rain at night. Temp. 2nd Lieut. J.G.J. Kidd - attached	qp
"	3	do. do. morning.	qp
"	4	do. Windy + some rain.	qp
"	5	do. Morning fine. Showers from noon.	qp
"	6	do.	qp On 31st January :- M.G. Detachment moved to QUESNOY to form part of Brigade M.G. Squadron, under command of Capt. E.J. Graves. Capt. M.M. Carpendale proceeded to command M.G. Squadron. qp
"	7	do.	qp
"	8	do. G.O.C. 1st Ind. Cav. Bdi. inspected "C" Sqn under Risaldar Sadiq. hund. much, carrying out a Tactical scheme. Rain all morning.	qp
"	9	do. Snowfall, one inch, early morning Frost at night.	qp
"	10	do. Fine all day.	qp
"	11	do. Rain. Cold.	qp
"	12	do. Stormy { Captain C.F. Cochrane sailed from MARSEILLES to join the Staff of Sir Percy Lake, Mesopotamia - qp	qp
"	13	do. do.	qp
"	14	do. do.	qp

Army Form C. 2118.

p. 89.

WAR DIARY of 38th Jacob's Horse.
INTELLIGENCE SUMMARY.
(Erase heading not required.)

Instructions regarding War Diaries and Intelligence Summaries are contained in F. S. Regs., Part II, and the Staff Manual respectively. Title pages will be prepared in manuscript.

Hour, Date, Place.		Summary of Events and Information.	Remarks and references to Appendices.
FRANLEU CAMPAGNE HYMMEVILLE FRIREULLES	Feb. 15.	Billets. High Wind. Rain afternoon & night.	Lieut M.E. Parnell appointed Adjutant from 1.2.16 vice Capt. C.F.Colmore
	16.	do. Rain all morning. Afternoon fine.	2nd Lieut. H.R. Lansdale (I.A.R.O) appointed Asst. Adjt. Qrmr. hostr. from 1.2.16.
	17.	do. Dry.	
	18.	do. Rain all day.	
	19.	do. Brigade Transport inspected by G.O.C. Division. Cold wind. Rain Eve.	
	20.	do. Sunshine all day. Slight frost at night.	
	21.	do. Cold & dull.	
	22.	do. Slight rain. Windy. Snow & frost at night.	Major W.G.K. Green, Officiating in Command, promoted to substve. Temp 2 rank of Lt. Col. to date from 25.12.15-
	23.	do. E. Wind. Very cold. 4 hours snow afternoon. Frost at night.	Lieut M.E. Parnell promoted Captain from 16.1.16
	24.	do. Sunshine. Hard frost at night.	
	25.	do. Snow blizzard from 11 am. till evening. 3 inches depth of snow. Frost at night.	
	26.	do. Dry.	
	27.	do. Thaw.	
	28.	do. Thaw continued. Rain. Digging Party rejoined from 7th Cavlm.	(Went away on 30th Jan.)
	29.	do. Morning fine. Evening rain.	

WGKGreen Lt.Col.
Comdg 38th Jacob's Horse.

Army Form C. 2118.

WAR DIARY
of 36th Jacob's Horse
1916.
INTELLIGENCE SUMMARY.
p. 88.

(Erase heading not required.)

Instructions regarding War Diaries and Intelligence Summaries are contained in F. S. Regs., Part II, and the Staff Manual respectively. Title pages will be prepared in manuscript.

Hour, Date, Place.		Summary of Events and Information.	Remarks and references to Appendices.
FRANLEU CAMPAGNE HYMMEVILLE FRIREULLES	Feb. 1	Billets. Dry. Cold wind.	On 30th January:— 1 J.O. + 56 men under comm. of 2nd Lieut. A.W. Harrison (J.J.R.) proceeded to 7th Corps for employment in defence works.
	" 2	do. Temp" 2nd Lieut. R. G. Faithfull attached.	
	" 3	do. Rain at night. Temp" 2nd Lieut J.G. Kidd attached	
	" 4	do. Windy + some rain.	
	" 5	do. Morning fine. Showers from noon.	
	" 6	do.	On 31st January:— M.G. detachment moved to QUESNOY to form part of Brigade M.G. Squadron, under command of Capt J. Graves. Capt. M.M. Carpendale proceeded to command M.G. Squadron.
	" 7	do.	
	" 8	do. G.O.C. 1st I.K. Cav. Bri. inspected "C" Sqn. under Rainlton Sadiq, hard march, carrying out a tactical scheme. Rain all morning.	
	" 9	do. Snowfall, one inch, early morning. Day fine. Frost at night.	
	" 10	do. Fine all day.	
	" 11	do. Rain. Cold.	
	" 12	do. do. Stormy { Captain C. F. Cochrane sailed from MARSEILLES to join the Staff of Sir. Percy Lake, Mesopotamia.	
	" 13	do. do.	
	" 14	do. do.	

Army Form C. 2118.

p. 89.

WAR DIARY
of 38th Jacob's Horse
1916.
INTELLIGENCE SUMMARY.
(Erase heading not required.)

Instructions regarding War Diaries and Intelligence Summaries are contained in F.S. Regs., Part II, and the Staff Manual respectively. Title pages will be prepared in manuscript.

Hour, Date, Place.			Summary of Events and Information.	Remarks and references to Appendices.
FRANLEU CAMPAGNE HYMMEVILLE FRIREULLES	Feb.	15.	Billets. High Wind. Rain afternoon & night.	Lieut M.E. Parnell, appointed Adjutant from 1.2.16 vice Capt. C.F. Clubrose.
		16.	do. Rain all morning. Afternoon fine.	2nd Lieut. H.R. Lonsdale (I.A.R.O) appointed officiating Quarter Master from 1.2.16.
		17.	do. Dry.	
		18.	do. Rain all day.	
		19.	do. Brigade Transport inspected by G.O.C. Division. Cold wind. Rain bar.d	
		20.	do. Sunshine all day. Slight frost at night.	
		21.	do. Cold & dull.	
		22.	do. Slight rain. Windy. Snow & frost at night.	
		23.	do. E. Wind. Very cold. 4 hours snow, afternoon. Frost at night.	Major W.G.K. Green, Officiating in Command, permitted to assume Temp.y rank of Lt. Col. to date from 25.12.15.
		24.	do. Sunshine. Hard frost at night.	Lieut M.E. Parnell promoted Captain from 16.1.16.
		25.	do. Snow blizzard from 11 a.m. till evening. 5 inches depth of snow. Frost at night.	
		26.	do. Dry.	
		27.	do. Thaw.	
		28.	do. Thaw continued. Rain. Digging Party rejoined from 7th Corps.	(Went away on 30th Jan.)
		29.	do. Morning fine. Evening, rain.	

W. Green. Lt. Col.
Comdg 38th Jacob's Horse.

Gulab Singh & Sons, Calcutta—No. 22 Army C.—5-8-14—1,07,000.

SERIAL No. 112

Confidential
Diary

of

36th Jacob's Horse.

FROM 1st March 1916 TO 31st March 1916.

Army Form C. 2118.

p. 90.

WAR DIARY of 36th Jacob's Horse.
INTELLIGENCE SUMMARY.

1916.

(Erase heading not required.)

Hour, Date, Place		Summary of Events and Information.	Remarks and references to Appendices.
FRANLEU	March. 1.	Billets. Fine. Capt. Simonds (35th H) rejoined from 1 month with Inf.y in Zurichen	ng.
CAMPAGNE	2.	" Morning fine. Evening, slight rain.	ng.
HYMMEVILLE	3.	" " slight rain.	ng.
FRIREULLES	4.	" Snow & rain.	ng.
	5.	" Fine.	ng.
	6.	" Snow early morning. 2nd Lt. E.N.E.Waldron I.A.R. rejoined.	ng.
	7.	" Frost at night. Day fine. Frost at night.	ng.
	8.	" do	ng.
	9.	" Morning bright. Slight snowfall at night.	ng.
	10.	" Snow disappeared.	ng.
	11.	" Capt. A.M.FORTEATH, 36th J.H. & 2nd Lt. D.B. EMERSON, I.A.R., joined the Regiment from the Base. Weather fine & dry.	ng.
	12.	" Sunshine all morning. Dry.	ng.
	13.	" do	ng.
	14.	" Morning bright. Heavy rain 9-10 p.m. The Lucknow Cavalry Bde. carried out Drills & manoeuvre on the sands N. of CAYEUX.	ng.
	15.	" Fine all day.	ng.
	16.	" Morning bright. Slight rain afternoon.	ng.

Army Form C. 2118.

P. 91.

WAR DIARY of 3rd Jacob's Horse
INTELLIGENCE SUMMARY.

(Erase heading not required.)

Instructions regarding War Diaries and Intelligence Summaries are contained in F. S. Regs., Part II, and the Staff Manual respectively. Title pages will be prepared in manuscript.

Hour, Date, Place.		Summary of Events and Information.	Remarks and references to Appendices.
FRANLEU CAMPAGNE HYMMEVILLE FRIEVULLES	March 17	Billets. Fine.	rg.
	" 18	Still. Slight rain afternoon.	rg.
	" 19	" Still.	rg.
	" 20	" Still - slight rain.	rg.
	" 21	" Col Lyser proceeds on leave. Maj Stanwell takes on command.	LOSR
	" 22	" Regtl drill for officers other than regular. Staff exercise movements executed by most of them. Some tactics evidently left desirable.	LOSR
		Orders re properties of promotions, examinations prescribed for reinforcements awaited for Brigade. Suggested 2 promotions from regt to 1 absorption of reinforcement.	LOSR
	" 23		LOSR
	" 24	Conference at G.O.C.s of all C.Os. Points attention was drawn to:—	LOSR
		(a) Better turn out of Indian troops in billets to be necessary.	
		(b) Saluting by all ranks, especially by I.A.R. Officers.	
		(c) Necessity of being courteous to ??? inhabitants in the billets we are sent to go to.	
		(d) Interest in supplies. B.O. to be stood off other duties especially to this. All supplies to be in one village.	
	" 25	Snow. March to new billets for ???.	LOSR

Army Form C. 2118.

P. 92

WAR DIARY

1916 of 36th Jacob's Horse

INTELLIGENCE SUMMARY.

(Erase heading not required.)

Hour, Date, Place.	Summary of Events and Information.	Remarks and references to Appendices.
March 26th BOUFFLERS and GENNE—IVERGNY via CANCHY and LE BOISLE	Started 8 am, drizzling rain and very cold. March later ½ hr earlier than necessary no fault of T.P. officer. Chiefly due to the fact all Indian ladies fond of being too early for parade. D.M. march in two stages. Pace and march discipline generally very good, but tendency to ride too much in middle of road. Inhabitants in new billets welcomed us. Bonos ate rather parched about owing to French mounted troops having been here for previous year. Horses out in open owing to risk of contagion of mange, like starting very wet and muddy, out pulling splendon. Activities great feeling to condition if this lasts long. H.Q., A, B, and HH at BOUFFLERS, C and D at GENNE IVERGNY. Accommodation for men good. D.M. in isolated barn.	S.S.M
March 27th	Heavy rain all night and showers at intervals throughout day. Men settling into billets. Conference at Regt H.Q. for Indian Com C.Os re reinforcements, their training and the proportion of I.O.s and N.C.Os. Result:— (a) Proportion of I.O.s and N.C.Os among reinforcements to be 25% of the Regtl establishment on agent 3.5% so it is hoped (b) One Officer to Depôt to begin to go to Marseilles to train reinforcements	

Army Form C. 2118.

P. 93

WAR DIARY

1916 of 36th Jacobs Horse

INTELLIGENCE SUMMARY.

(Erase heading not required.)

Instructions regarding War Diaries and Intelligence Summaries are contained in F. S. Regs., Part II, and the Staff Manual respectively. Title pages will be prepared in manuscript.

Hour, Date, Place.	Summary of Events and Information.	Remarks and references to Appendices.
March 25th	Rain all night. Horse standings absolute quagmire. In case of A sqdn. (A.B.D. Sqdns had their lines pitched in flat meadow in valley close to R. AUTHIE). Shifted A sqdn to inside & round on top of hill, standing good and shelters from wind.	C.O.C
	Sun cleaning up horse billets in view of terrible sanitation to put animals under cover. In most cases those were filthy, nearly a foot deep in dung.	
March 29th	Inspection of billets by Gen Fasken. Regt complimented on cleanliness of billets and good work put in towards cleaning out horse standings at Colonel Lynn to be informed of G.O.C.s satisfaction & progress and general improvement during his term of command.	C.O.C
	Got in letter suggesting advisability of having a Cavalry Pioneer Course.	
	Col Lynn returned from leave.	
	Fine day, but rather cold.	
March 30th	Ground dried up considerably.	
March 31st	Fine day. Bright sunshine. Horse standings much improved.	

W. Lyon Lt.Col.
Comdg. 36th Jacobs Horse

SERIAL NO. 112.

Confidential

War Diary

of

36th Jacob's Horse.

FROM 1st April 1916 TO 30th April 1916.

Army Form C. 2118.

P. 94

WAR DIARY
of 36th Jacob's Horse
1916
INTELLIGENCE SUMMARY.

(Erase heading not required.)

Instructions regarding War Diaries and Intelligence Summaries are contained in F.S. Regs., Part II, and the Staff Manual respectively. Title pages will be prepared in manuscript.

Hour, Date, Place.	Summary of Events and Information.	Remarks and references to Appendices.
April 1st BOUFFLERS and GENNE-IVERGNY	Lt.Col. Grew and two other combatant* proceed on a reconnaissance. (also 1 M.G. Officer, Lieut. F.B. Maltby) Fine day	*Capt. F.K. Farquhar " W.F. Blacker C.O.S.
April 2nd	Fine warm day	C.O.S.
April 3rd	Parade & repeater drill for all I.A.R. officers under Captain FORTEATH. Lts HARRISON, EMERSON and BRAITHWAITE know something about it – reminder required some practice.	C.O.S.
April 4th	Wood-fighting scheme near LABROYE. Following mistakes: (a) advance far to extend (b) sections completely lost touch of each other (c) direction lost (d) tendency of men & even officers to get excited and beyond control. "enemy" ably handled by Lt HARRISON Fine day, rather fresh out chilly in evening Lt.Col. Green & reconnoitring party (3 Br. Officers + 10 men) joined in the evening ⊕ work done: Reconnaissance of portion of Corps & Army Defences in 6th Corps area & road leading there to. Distance covered on return journey in one day 41 miles.	⊕ Captain Blacker rejoined independently on 2.4.16 to attend Hotchkiss Gun Instructional Course with Sialkot Car Bde. AB.

Army Form O. 2118.

WAR DIARY

INTELLIGENCE SUMMARY

1916 of 38th Jacob's Horse

P 95

Instructions regarding War Diaries and Intelligence Summaries are contained in F. S. Regs., Part II, and the Staff Manual respectively. Title pages will be prepared in manuscript.

(Erase heading not required.)

Hour, Date, Place.	Summary of Events and Information.	Remarks and references to Appendices.
BOUFFLERS and GENNE-IVERGNY. April 5.	Still + cold. I.A.R. Officers gave instruction in Sqn. drill by Capt. Forteath.	ng.
6	Extracts from Gazette of India dated 3rd March 1916:— Lieut. W. F. Blacker to be Captain from 2 March, 1916. Capt. H. Maurice to be Temp. Major in the 2nd Queens R.W. Surrey Regt. from 29 Nov. 1915. Intimation received that Lieut.Col. R.E. Rowe is permitted to vacate command of the Regt. from 18.2.16 (sick)	ng. ng.
7.	Still early — Sunshine later.	ng.
8.	Sunshine, morning.	ng. 3 Hotchkiss Guns arrived, first instalment of the 16 with which each regiment is to be equipped.
GAPENNES. April 9.	The Regiment marched to GAPENNES (7 miles) + went into billets there, for a week, to take part in Brigade training over an area specially allotted for the purpose. Weather fine.	ng.
10.	Squadron + Regimental Training. Good opportunity for many weeks. Day fine. 1 Regimental drill.	ng.
11.	Weather changed suddenly to strong gale with heavy rain. Squadron + Regimental drill in morning. Brigade drill + manoeuvre in afternoon.	ng.

Army Form C. 2118.

p. 96.

WAR DIARY
6th Jacob's Horse
1916
INTELLIGENCE SUMMARY.
(Erase heading not required.)

Instructions regarding War Diaries and Intelligence Summaries are contained in F. S. Regs., Part II, and the Staff Manual respectively. Title pages will be prepared in manuscript.

Hour, Date, Place.		Summary of Events and Information.	Remarks and references to Appendices.
GAPENNES	April 12.	Morning:- Brigade Tactical Exercise (Mounted pursuit) with Ball Ammunition. Violent wind. Rain in afternoon.	AB
	13.	Morning:- Brigade Tactical Exercise. Brigade acting as Flank Guard to an Infantry force advancing. Regt. detailed as Adv. Gd. to the Brigade. Proceeding's culminated in dismounted attack on small force of Infantry in position. Very heavy rain all day.	AB
	14.	Morning: Regimental Drill, followed by exhibition of a German Flammenwerfer in action against trenches, demonstrating practically that flames can do no harm to men keeping well down in trenches, nor to men standing in the open at 30 yards' distance. Weather: Stormy but no rain till evening. The horses which had suffered much from being picketted in open outside boundary of village were brought into the village & picketted in farm yards &c, to shelter them from wind.	
	15.	Morning: Brigade Tactical Exercise. Passing over enemy's captured Trench lines + digging in a position to assist in Keeping gap open. Afternoon: Marched back to former billets. Strong wind { a few showers.	AB
BOUFFLERS + GENNE-IVERGNY.			AB

Army Form C. 2118.

p. 97.

WAR DIARY
36th Jacob's Horse
1916.
INTELLIGENCE SUMMARY.
(Erase heading not required.)

Hour, Date, Place.	Summary of Events and Information.	Remarks and references to Appendices.
BOUFFLERS GENNE-IVERGNY Apr. 16.	Morning bright. Afternoon dull + cold.	a
17.	Stormy + wet. Horse standings deep in mud. Hotchkiss Gun Class commenced under Captn. Blacker.	a b. { 3 more Hotchkiss Guns arrived: Total 6.
18.	All buildings which had held French cavalry horses disinfected.	c. All officers men on leave recalled by 18th.
19.	Storm + rain continued — Horses still standing outside. Storm + rain continued — disinfecting building passed by Veterinary Officer: all animals, except those of Transport establishment, put under cover in afternoon. Very wet night.	d.
20.	Showers at intervals. Storm abated.	a.
21.	Regiment proceeded to Training ground, S. of YVRENCH, to drill in afternoon, returning to billets in evening. Evening very wet. 1st Hotchkiss Gun Class, under Captn. Blacker, ended — Officers instructed: Lieut. Harrison (A) " Walsh (B) " Brookmonte (C) " Emerson (A) Resr. Rissldr. Ayub (B)	a. These Officers are to commence classes in their respective Sqns. on the 24th April.
22.	Very wet all day.	a.
23.	Complete change in weather. Fine all day.	a.
24.	Fine all day.	a.
	2nd Lieut. R.G. Faithfull (Reserve Cav., attached) commenced a week's course in the Hotchkiss Automatic Rifle at the 1st Ind. Cav. Divisional School.	a.

Army Form O. 2118.

p. 98.

WAR DIARY of 36th Jacob's Horse
INTELLIGENCE SUMMARY.
1916

(Erase heading not required.)

Hour, Date, Place.	Summary of Events and Information.	Remarks and references to Appendices.
BOUFFLERS } April 25. GENNE-IVERGNY }	Fine weather continued.	
26.	Regiment proceeded to usual Training Ground, S. of YVRENCH, in morning for drills; returning in afternoon. Fine - warm.	
27.	Fine - warm.	
28.	All available British + Indian Officers attended a Regimental Tactical Exercise, between GENNE-IVERGNY + QUOEUX. Warm, slight breeze.	
29.	Regiment proceeded in morning for drill under the Adjutant on usual portion of training ground. C.O. + all Squadron Commdrs. taken as Umpires in a Divisional Field Day (2 Brigades.) Day fine; strong easterly breeze.	
30.		

W. Green Lt. Col.
Commdg. 36th Jacob's Horse.

SERIAL NO. 112.

Confidential
War Diary
of
36th Jacob's Horse

FROM 1st May 1916 TO 31st May 1916.

Army Form C. 2118.

p. 99.

WAR DIARY
of 30 Jacob's Horse
INTELLIGENCE SUMMARY.
(Erase heading not required.)

Hour, Date, Place.		Summary of Events and Information.	Remarks and references to Appendices.
BOUFFLERS GENNE-IVERGNY —— ST RIQUIER.	May 1.	The Regiment, less dismounted Men, Sick men & Sick Horses, marched to temporary billets at ST RIQUIER, to take part in a weeks Divisional Training in the Training area. Fine - Few showers in evening	1st May 2nd Lieuts. Kidd & Lonsdale Commenced courses at the Divisional School: 2/Lt. Kidd, 1 week Hotchkiss Auto. Rifle. 2/Lt Lonsdale, 3 days, Gassing.
"	2.	Divisional Tactical Exercise 7am to 1 pm. Thunderstorm & hail 10 am - Some rain during afternoon. The other 2 Brigades of The Division (Sialkot & Mhow) are also billeted in neighbourhood of Training Area.	
"	3.	Divisional Tactical Exercise 7.30 am to 3 pm. Cloudy & cold in morning - Afternoon sunshine.	
"	4.	Divisional Tactical Exercise under inspection of Lt. Gen-l Sir H. Gough. Fine day.	
"	5.	Brigade Tact. Exe - without troops. Weather very summery.	
"	6.	Divisional Tactical Exercises - Repetition of Scheme for 4th May. Weather fresh, fine generally, 2 short showers. Some rain at night.	
BOUFFLERS GENNE-IVERGNY	7.	Regiment returned to permanent billets BOUFFLERS + GENNE-IVERGNY - Training Area was vacated today by the whole of the 1st J.C.D. Rain at intervals throughout day.	8th May 2nd Lieut. Lonsdale (for sniping) " Harrison (for Hotchkiss Rifle) proceed to Divisional School for 1 weeks course.
"	8.	Showers morning - Fine afternoon. Strong wind. Very cold	
"	9.	Rain throughout day, heavy at night.	

Army Form C. 2118.

p. 100.

WAR DIARY
of 36 Jacob's Horse
1916
INTELLIGENCE SUMMARY.
(Erase heading not required.)

Instructions regarding War Diaries and Intelligence Summaries are contained in F. S. Regs., Part II, and the Staff Manual respectively. Title pages will be prepared in manuscript.

Hour, Date, Place.	Summary of Events and Information.	Remarks and references to Appendices.
MONCHEAUX. May.10.	Regiment marched to new billets at MONCHEAUX. Whole Regiment in same village; most of the horses picketted outside. Barns for accommodation of men generally very good & roomy. Officers' billets fair to good. Lucknow Brigade Area:— REBREUVE (N⁰ Q⁰), CAN-ETTEMONT (29ᵗʰ L⁰ʳˢ) SERICOURT-SIBIVILLE (K.D.G.) MONCHEAUX (36ᵗʰ J.H.) HONVAL (M.G. Sqn + M.V.S.) — "U" R.H.A., & Jodhpur Lancers in REBREUVE. Day fine: after" bright - cold.	NB.
11.	Pack equipment for 6 Hotchkiss Automatic Rifles who received today. This is to be given a thorough trial before it is reported on.	NB.
12.	Weather: dull; cold; some sunshine in evening.	NB.
13.	do. Still - Dry.	NB.
	do. Heavy rain, morning.	
14.	Command of Lucknow Cavalry Brigade was taken over today by Brig⁰ General Gage. Jemadar Abu Khan went to England on a visit, with a party of Indian Officers from the 1ˢᵗ Indian Cavalry Division, conducted to London by Captain W. F. Blacker.	NB.
15	Weather: dull, evening cold, night stormy. Ress: Major Muk⁰ᵈ Nasir Khan & Jem" Angun Gul departed for India for transfer to Pension Establishment. Heavy rain, morning; Cold, night fine	NB. 2 W. L.O. Chwith & Braithwaite & 8 N.C.O.s went to Divisional School for a week's course in bombing & Hotchkiss auto" rifle.

Gulab Singh & Sons, Calcutta—No. 22 Army—5.8.14—1,07,000.

Army Form C. 2118.

p. 101.

WAR DIARY

of 36th ~~Jacob's~~ Horse

1916

INTELLIGENCE SUMMARY.

(Erase heading not required.)

Instructions regarding War Diaries and Intelligence Summaries are contained in F. S. Regs., Part II, and the Staff Manual respectively. Title pages will be prepared in manuscript.

Hour, Date, Place.	Summary of Events and Information.	Remarks and references to Appendices.
MONCHEAUX. May 16, 17.	Weather: Bright sunshine, warm.	g.
18.	Jem: Encha Singh departed for India, to take up appointment of Wordi Major at depot.	g.
19-22	Fine + hot weather continued till mid-day 22nd, when sky became clouded + temperature fell. Bright rain showers evening.	g.
23	2 Lieuts Ogley + Emerson commenced classes at Divisional School (Bombing + Sniping) for 1 week. Weather fine, hot, thundery.	g.
24, 25	Heavy rain.	g.
26-28	Fine weather.	g.
29-30	Rain night 29th + early morning 30th. Day fine, night cold.	g.
31	Day fine - night very cold.	g.

[signature]
Comdg. 36th Jacob's Horse.

SERIAL NO. 112.

Confidential
Diary
of

36th Jacob's Horse.

FROM 1st June 1916 TO 30th June 1916.

Army Form C. 2118.

p. 102.

WAR DIARY of 36th Jacob's Horse
INTELLIGENCE SUMMARY.

1916.

(Erase heading not required.)

Instructions regarding War Diaries and Intelligence Summaries are contained in F. S. Regs., Part II, and the Staff Manual respectively. Title pages will be prepared in manuscript.

Hour, Date, Place.	Summary of Events and Information.	Remarks and references to Appendices.
MONCHEAUX; June, 1.	Weather dull – No rain – Night clear + cold ; strong wind.	Note :– 26th May; 2nd Lieut. A.E.F. Wood, I.A.R. joined the Regt. from Base.
2.	Fine.	
3.	Showers in morning. Evening + night very cold.	
4.	Cold wind all day. Steady rain all night.	
5.	Major H.M. Saunderson rejoined Regt. from Temp'y duty with a Service Batt. (20th Lancers. Tiwana) of which he had been 2nd in Comm'd since Nov. 1915. Lieut. C. Sleand joined Div'l School for week's course, Hotchkiss A.R.	
6.	Weather :– Heavy rain 10 a.m. Cold windy afternoon.	
7.	do :– Heavy rain morning.	7th Lieut. K.F. Channer + 100 reinforcements arriving at Base from India.
8.	do :– Showers morning. Heavy rain all night.	
9.	do :– Sunshine morning. Bright later.	
10.	do :– Some showers.	
	Ressaldar Muhamed Hayit Khan + 19 men joined from Base	
11–15	Weather :– Showers morning. Heavy rain afternoon.	
16, 17	" Rain each day; several heavy showers. Still + cold generally.	
18	" Fine, Cold. Fine. Sunshine.	
19	6 Br.Off'rs. 8 I.Off'rs. + 286 Rank + file under Comm'd of Major Maunsell went up in lorries to MONT ST.ELOY for work near front line Trenches. Weather :– Dropping rain noon + evening. 4 Hotchkiss Automatic Rifles + Teams (12 men) sent up to join above working party.	Maj. Maunsell / Lt. Faithfull Capt. Renshaw " Kidd Lieut. Christie " Wood.

Gulab Singh & Sons, Calcutta—No. 52 Army C—5-8-14—1,07,000.

Army Form C. 2118.

P 103

WAR DIARY
of 36th Jacob's Horse
INTELLIGENCE SUMMARY
1916

(Erase heading not required.)

Instructions regarding War Diaries and Intelligence Summaries are contained in F. S. Regs., Part II, and the Staff Manual respectively. Title pages will be prepared in manuscript.

Hour, Date, Place.	Summary of Events and Information.	Remarks and references to Appendices.
	Diary of digging party under Major Darwell	
June 18th	Arrived ST ELOI 6.0 p.m. Uncomfortable night in dirty huts. Weather fine	cost
June 19th	Maj. Darwell and Lieut Cubbe took over defensive sector of NEUVILLE ST VAAST Regiment marched out from ST ELOI 9.30 p.m. via LA TARGETTE road, no shelling en route. Took over dug outs and fatigue parties by 1 a.m. Owing to the system of trenches being a regular maze the men slept in alarm posts instead of in dug outs. Working parties were employed in mine shafts. About 2 a.m. mine was exploded by Germans and an attack seemed imminent. Coy Commanders of British Infantry in whose sector of front line the men were working reported that the men had shown great steadiness and had been of great assistance. despite the fact that they had no Bristol stores with	cost

Army Form C. 2118.

P. 104

WAR DIARY
of 2nd Jacob's Horse
1916
INTELLIGENCE SUMMARY.
(Erase heading not required.)

Hour, Date, Place.	Summary of Events and Information.	Remarks and references to Appendices.
June 20=	There are no known Hindustanis to explain to them what was wanted. (N.B. The men were unfit in parties of 100-150 only and was not expect in but line trenches) and were greatly rattled about. I rate detailed reconnaissance of the perimeter of NEUVILLE be which regret was refused — but 1500 yds will about 100 men and 4 Hotchkiss rifles to hold it. Practised "attack quarters" in afternoon. Area in most filthy condition — accumulating of rubbish and debris in every direction. Some shelling in morning but no casualties. Ressaidar Mohd NUR and 7 men D sqdn. Pluckily rescued some Sappers who had been overcome by CO gas in a mine shaft. Commenced improving communication trenches in night portion of sector. Men having casualties would be incurred in getting men out to "attack quarters" would be very much affected about. Men working under it there was shelled about.	E.B.S.

Army Form C. 2118.

P. 105

WAR DIARY
of 36th Jacobs Horse
INTELLIGENCE SUMMARY.

1916

(Erase heading not required.)

Instructions regarding War Diaries and Intelligence Summaries are contained in F. S. Regs., Part II, and the Staff Manual respectively. Title pages will be prepared in manuscript.

Hour, Date, Place.	Summary of Events and Information.	Remarks and references to Appendices.
June 21st	Suffers work to pm on and got 16 hours off. Practically whole regiment employed in this manner.	
NEUVILLE ST VAAST in morning	Detailed reconnaissance of Hotchkiss gun position walks to future them. Owing to lack of men was continued improvement in right sector out opened of communication trenches & to futeteen to exit from obsg onto in left sector. One shell burst by men kitchen and one by Dugdr cookhouse but fortunately no casualties. Lt WOOD was found night – but his tracks. Heavy thunderstorm. Trenches flooded in parts.	(GS)

Army Form C. 2118.

WAR DIARY
or
INTELLIGENCE SUMMARY
(Erase heading not required.)

19 ___ 36th Jacob Horse

P.106

Place	Date	Hour	Summary of Events and Information	Remarks and references to Appendices
NEUVILLE ST VAAST	Jan 22nd		Continued improvement of communication trenches in right sector. Arranged drainage of trenches that were flooded. This involved a lot of labour. Party reconnoitring to establish position at Nord of NEUVILLE were shelled in the evening. Fortunately no casualties. Our guns shelled enemy heavily at intervals throughout the day — patrolling towards NEUVILLE.	COSY
	23rd		Dull day. About 2 am enemy opened fire on NEUVILLE. Heavy shell fire on firing line & R.E. close to and towards a pile of rondelays erected by R.E. close to and Dugouts. She fire lasted about an hour when our guns, whilst were in great proximity, silenced him. As all the men were in part proximity, silenced him. As all the men went either out of the area or making patrois or were in their dug outs or were hit. Had "stick grenades" been about the casualties would have been very heavy. Continued improvement of C. Trenches in right sector & work on protection & revets from dug outs in left sector. Dull day. Showers at intervals.	LOST

Army Form C. 2118.

WAR DIARY of INTELLIGENCE SUMMARY

1916 36th Jacob's Horse

(Erase heading not required.)

P. 107

Place	Date	Hour	Summary of Events and Information	Remarks and references to Appendices
NEUVILLE ST VAAST	24th		Had store wells out thanks now well un night sector. Brightened out altogether. A lot of men congregate here away at odd hours of the day out a lucky shell might do a lot of damage. Pressed some Hotchkiss enplacements, and carried on improvement of protection to exits from dugouts in left sector. A few shells burst in the area but inflicted no casualties. Owing to revisions to working tables we are about 180 rifles ourselves available for defence. Heavy ½ gunfire on hostile trenches towards THELUS and NW of LA FOLIE FARM, enemy retired with 5.9 but was unable to locate our batteries. At 11.30 hrs division on our left carried out miniature raid a little trench. Enemy retaliated with gunfire on and sent some shell into NEUVILLE. Ration parties but carriers made from a shell. Drizzly and dull day.	
	25th		Internal communication trenches in right sector and carried on. Protection to exits from dugouts in left sector. Stole two new Hotchkiss	

Army Form C. 2118.

WAR DIARY
of 36th Jacob's Horse
INTELLIGENCE SUMMARY
(Erase heading not required.)

P. 108

Place	Date	Hour	Summary of Events and Information	Remarks and references to Appendices
NEUVILLE ST VAAST	26th		replacements and burial. A. Had some patrols & the accumulated filth cleared away, and buried. Carried protective work in little sectors. Had more good luck. Some shells burst in night sector — no casualties.	LOST
	27th		Advance party of 2/13 Foster Regt came in to take over trenches at 5.0 pm. As however men were to go out on working parties as well as cleaning of the area, which is still pretty filthy. Some shelling early in the morning. Reliefs began to arrive in batches about 12.0 noon, very intermittent as they had to walk out mostly at communication trenches, arranged for our men to do a short shift for them until they had rested but they were not contemplated. Relief completed at 8.0 pm when our last party marched for ST ELOI.	LOST
			ST ELOI. Uncomfortable night in huts at ST ELOI.	

Army Form C. 2118.

P. 109

WAR DIARY
of 36th Jacob's Horse
INTELLIGENCE SUMMARY

(Erase heading not required.)

Instructions regarding War Diaries and Intelligence Summaries are contained in F.S. Regs., Part II. and the Staff Manual respectively. Title Pages will be prepared in manuscript.

Place	Date	Hour	Summary of Events and Information	Remarks and references to Appendices
MONCHEAUX	28th		Entrained at ST ELOI at 5.0 am and returned to MONCHEAUX	(App I)
	29th		Dull day	(App I)
			Inspection by G.O.C. in Marching order. Transport loaded according to war scale. (App I.)	(App I)
BOUT DES PRES	30th		Marched to BOUT DES PRES 3 miles N of DOULLENS	

C.D. Naumwell Major
30.6.16

SERIAL NO. 112

Confidential

War Diary

of

3.6th Jacob's Horse

FROM 1st July 1916 TO 31st July 1916

WAR DIARY
or
INTELLIGENCE SUMMARY

of 7 36th Jacob's Horse

(Erase heading not required.)

Army Form C. 2118.

p. 110

1916

Place	Date 1916	Hour	Summary of Events and Information	Remarks and references to Appendices
BOUT DES PRES	July 1.		In close billets. K.D.G's in GROUCHES, 29th Lancers in MILLY; Bde. H.Q., GROUCHES. Weather; Fine, hot.	AB
	2.	3.30 p.m. 5 p.m.	Received notice that Division was to move today. Orders received to move at 6 p.m. Brigade moved to new area as follows:- Bde. H.Q. + K.D.Gs at FROHEN-le-Grand, M.G. Sqn. at FROHEN-le-petit., 36th J.H. + 29th L. at VILLIERS-L'HOPITAL. Arrived new billets 9 p.m. Weather; bright + warm by day, bright cold.	AB
VILLERS L'HOPITAL.	3.		2nd Lieut. E.N.E. Waldron, I.A.R.O., directed to join balloon sect. R.F.C. as a probationer observing officer. Brigade is on 2½ hours notice. Billeting parties are warned to be ready to move at a moments notice. Weather; Bright + warm. Rain, night.	AB
	4 to 16		Regiment remained in same billets. Period occupied in Regimental + Brigade training. — Tactical exercises, swimming horses + improvised bridging, competitions, field firing + harrying of Hotchkiss automatic rifle teams. 2nd Lieut. J. G. Kidd (11th Res. Cav.) transferred to R.F.C. on probation, on 7.7.15. Lieut. K. F. Chanmer joined The Regt. from Base on 9.7.15. Weather. Heavy rain on 4th + 7th. Slight showers on 6th, 12th, 13th, 16th. Remaining days fine to cloudy. Steady rain evening of 15th. Division was put back to 8 hours notice for a move on 11th.	AB

Army Form C. 2118.

WAR DIARY
of 36th Jacob's Horse
INTELLIGENCE SUMMARY
1916

(Erase heading not required.)

Instructions regarding War Diaries and Intelligence Summaries are contained in F.S. Regs., Part II and the Staff Manual respectively. Title Pages will be prepared in manuscript.

Place	Date	Hour	Summary of Events and Information	Remarks and references to Appendices
VILLERS L'HOPITAL	July 17-18	—	Rain afternoon 17th & morning 18th.	
VILLERS BRULIN	19.	—	On change of Division, Billeting area. Regiment marched to VILLERS BRULIN (12 miles N.N.W. of ARRAS) distance 20 miles; whole Regt. billeted in this village. Brigade H.Q., VILLERS BRULIN; K.D.G.s & 29th L.s, CAMBLIGNEUL; M.G. Sqn. & Mob. Vet.y. Secn., BETHENCOURT. Weather fine.	A. A.
	20.	1.30p	The following party, under command of Captn. Farquhar, proceeded, dismounted, to MARŒUIL for work in front line trenches near ROCLINCOURT: 5 British officers (Lts. Sleaye, Braithwaite, Landale, Ogley & Emerson — all I.A.R. Officers), S.I.O.s & 303 other ranks. Weather fine - bright.	A.
	21-25		Weather hazy to cloudy. Slight drizzle morning of 25th. Remainder of Regt. in billets fully occupied in exercise & care of horses. Training in trot & knee limits; rifle kept up.	A.
	26-31		Weather: 26th. Dull - a little fine rain. 27th - 29th. Morning misty remainder of day fine & hot. 30th, 31st. Bright & hot.	A.
	30.		Trench working party rejoined Regiment at VILLERS BRULIN between afternoon & midnight in two portions. Total Casualties: 1 Killed (Sr. Murt. Ali, 23rd Cav. F.F., B.Sqn.), 2 wounded by falling timber (Sikhs — since returned to duty), 1 Sr. accidentally wounded.	?

A.E. Green Lt.Col.
Comdg. 36th Jacob's Horse.

2449 Wt. W14957/M90 750,000 1/16 J.B.C. & A. Forms/C.2118/12.

SERIAL NO. 112.

Confidential
War Diary
of

36th Jacob's Horse.

FROM 1st August 1916 TO 31st August 1916.

Army Form C. 2118.

WAR DIARY
of 36th JACOB'S HORSE
INTELLIGENCE SUMMARY
1916
(Erase heading not required.)

Instructions regarding War Diaries and Intelligence Summaries are contained in F.S. Regs., Part II. and the Staff Manual respectively. Title Pages will be prepared in manuscript.

p.112

Place	Date 1916	Hour	Summary of Events and Information	Remarks and references to Appendices
VILLERS BRULIN	Aug. 1-7		Billets - VILLERS BRULIN.	AB
	8.		A Composite Squadron, made up of 1 strong troop from each of the 4 Squadrons, moved to billets at GAUCHIN, near ST POL, on Special Escort duty to H.I.M. the King + H.R.H. the Prince of Wales, on a visit to the Armies in France. Strength:— B.O.'s 3 (Major Davidson, Capt. Poujalin, Lieut. Chauvin) I.O.'s 4 (R.M. Bagga Singh, Risaldar Sadiq Mmd.+ Mmd. ot Nizam Khan, Ress. Mohd Kh, Mmd. ot Khan.) B. Ranks 146 I. Ranks 146	2nd/Lt HOWELL (Punjab Lt Horse attached) arrived at GAUDIEMPRE on 8th to join the Regiment. AB
	9.		Brigade moved to new area about PAS, to furnish working parties in trench line of the VII Corps.— Lnshen or Car. Bole. H.Q. at PAS. The Regiment (less the Composite Squadron) marched from VILLERS BRULIN at 9.30 a.m. + arrived at its new billets, GAUDIEMPRE, at 2.30 p.m. having stopped to water at BARLY en route. (Note:- There is no water in the River G.Y. where it crosses the AVESNES-LE-COMTE — BARLY road. Though the stream is distinctly marked in blue on the map — LENS 1/100000.)	AB
GAUDIEMPRE	10.	9 am.	A working party of 7 B.O.'s, 3 I.O.'s, 3 B.R.'s, 271 I. Rks. + 4 followers, motor command of Capt. J.W. Emond, marched on foot to huts at SOUASTRE, for carrying duties in trenches for 3 nights.	AB

2449 Wt. W14957/Mg0 750,000 1/16 J.B.C. & A. Forms/C.2118/12.

Army Form C. 2118.

WAR DIARY
of 36th Jacob's Horse
INTELLIGENCE SUMMARY
1916
(Erase heading not required.)

p.113.

Instructions regarding War Diaries and Intelligence Summaries are contained in F. S. Regs., Part II. and the Staff Manual respectively. Title Pages will be prepared in manuscript.

Place	Date 1916 August	Hour	Summary of Events and Information	Remarks and references to Appendices
GAUDIEMPRE	13.	3 p.m.	The Trench working Party rejoined the Regiment from SOUASTRE, after completion of the 3 nights' carrying work. No Casualties. The weather was fine throughout & the party had roomy, clean huts, for their billets just outside the village of SOUASTRE, S.E. end. Lieut. EMERSON, (I.A.R.), Jemadar NUR KHAN, + 8 Snipers (B.& D. Sqn. men) were despatched to BIENVILLERS (billets) for practice in patrolling + sniping from front line trenches.	A. Indelible Pencil. B. E.E. Section.
COULLEMONT	21.	10 a.m.	Regt. moved to new billets in COULLEMONT, owing to GAUDIEMPRE being over full of troops + the horse standings crowded, + deep in mud from heavy rain during past week. 29th Lancers also moved today, from WARLINCOURT to WARLUZEL. The K.D.G.s + M.G. Sqdron remained at HUMBERCOURT + Brigade H.Q. at PAS. Following party left for 1 week's work (Tunnelling) in the Trenches; billets in BIENVILLERS:- Major Davidson; Lieuts: Dablin, Braithwaite + Faithfull + Indian Officers. 150 Other ranks, plus Cooks + Batmen.	Lieutenant Emerson Bath Camp of the 36th Jacob's Horse
	22.		Also from today, for 1 week, the Regiment furnishes a working party of 150 men daily for making fascines, hurdles + prisoner fagots in the FORET de LUCHEUX - working hours 9 a.m. to 4 p.m. the party rides to the forest in the morning + marches back to billets on foot in the evening, distance 3½ to 4 miles.	Capt. Flint Offg. Comdg.

Army Form C. 2118.

p.114.

WAR DIARY
1916   36th Jacob's Horse
or
INTELLIGENCE SUMMARY

(Erase heading not required.)

Instructions regarding War Diaries and Intelligence Summaries are contained in F. S. Regs., Part II. and the Staff Manual respectively. Title Pages will be prepared in manuscript.

Place	Date 1916	Hour	Summary of Events and Information	Remarks and references to Appendices
COULEMONT	Aug 29.	Eveng	The Trench working party under Major Davidson & Snipers under Lieut. Emerson rejoined Hd Qrs from BIENVILLERS.	NB.

WHGreenfield.
Com'g 36th Jacob's Horse.
31. Aug. 1916.

2449 Wt. W14957/M90 750,000 1/16 J.B.C. & A. Forms/C.2118/12.

SERIAL NO. 112

Confidential War Diary

of

36. Jacob's Horse

FROM 1st September 1916 TO 30th September 1916

Army Form C. 2118.

P. 115

WAR DIARY
of 15 Jacob's Horse

1916.

INTELLIGENCE SUMMARY

(Erase heading not required.)

Instructions regarding War Diaries and Intelligence Summaries are contained in F. S. Regs., Part II. and the Staff Manual respectively. Title Pages will be prepared in manuscript.

Place	Date 1916	Hour	Summary of Events and Information	Remarks and references to Appendices
COULLEMONT	Septr 1-2		In billets at COULLEMONT.	AB.
REMAISNIL	3.		Lucknow Cavalry Brigade left its billeting area to join divisional concentration for training in the ST. RIQUIER training area. The Regiment marched, in Brigade, to REMAISNIL, where it billeted for the night.	AB.
GAPENNES	4.		Continued its march & went into billets at GAPENNES, N. of ST. RIQUIER. — This is the second occasion on which the Regt. was billeted in this village.	AB.
BEAUVOIR RIVIERE	11		The 1st Indian Cavalry Division commenced its move to the Cavalry concentration on the SOMME battle front, brigades marching independently. Regiment billeted for the night in BEAUVOIR RIVIERE on the R. AUTHIE.	AB.
HEM	12.		Moved to billets at HEM, near DOULLENS.	AB.
QUERRIEU	13.		Today the whole Division marched together, in the order Mhow, Lucknow, Sialkot; each Brigade's "A" Echelon transport following its own Brigade. The Division bivouacked on open ground to N. of QUERRIEU, E.N.E of AMIENS. Lucknow Brigade reached the bivouac 7 p.m. Heavy rain fell for about an hour (9 p.m.) but remainder of night was dry & the ground cold.	AB.

Army Form C. 2118.

WAR DIARY of 35th Jacob's Horse
INTELLIGENCE SUMMARY
1916
p.116

(Erase heading not required.)

Instructions regarding War Diaries and Intelligence Summaries are contained in F. S. Regs., Part II. and the Staff Manual respectively. Title Pages will be prepared in manuscript.

Place	Date 1916	Hour	Summary of Events and Information	Remarks and references to Appendices
QUERRIEU	Sept 14		Division remained in bivouac in QUERRIEU Camp. Any day + fine but a very cold N. wind blowing.	AB
VILLE-SOUS-CORBIE SERNANCOURT	15.	5 a.m.	Lucknow Brigade moved across the river beside camp + marched to VILLE-SOUS-CORBIE, preceded by Mhow + followed by Sialkot brigades. —AERANCOURT. Whole Division bivouacked in close area. Bivouac reached at 11 a.m. Orders were received for 2nd in Comd. of Regt. + 2nd in Comd. of Squadrons to remain behind at commencement of operations, as a reserve with "A" Echelon Transport. { This order was readjusted later + the total number to accompany the Regt. was limited to 12. The 2nd in Comd. will not accompany the Regt. }	AB
	16		All the Officers in turn went on reconnaissance to learn the routes + tracks that had been prepared across the trenches on the SOMME Battlefield, and the site of the (now generally) "D" Squadron (Major Davidson + Lieut. Emerson) moved up to MAMETZ by 7 a.m., with tools + ambulances, no short squadron for the day, under orders of XV Corps. They were not called upon to do any work + returned to Regiments Bivouac at 8 p.m.	AB
	17		do.	AB
	18-22		do.	AB
	23		do.	AB
			Heavy rain from 6th(?) Sept(?) to morning of 31st turned the camps into a bog for	AB

Army Form C. 2118.

WAR DIARY of 36th Jacob's Horse
INTELLIGENCE SUMMARY
(Erase heading not required.)

1916
p. 117.

Place	Date	Hour	Summary of Events and Information	Remarks and references to Appendices
DERNANCOURT	1916 Sept 24		Several days. The tracks prepared for the Cavalry across the battle field were almost impassable in many places. From 21st onwards there was fine weather.	
	25		The tracks were gradually dried up. Same bivouac.	
			Lucknow Brigade held in reserve for possible Cavalry operations; MHow do. + Sialkot Brigades having moved up & formed position of readiness at 1300 de BERM & FAY & MAMETZ respectively. The Regiment was kept at 1 hours notice for a move till 9 p.m. when it was put on to 3 hours notice. Between 9 + 10 p.m. hostile aeroplanes passed over the Cavalry camps area dropping bombs. The 3rd Hussars alone suffered casualties (10 horses & 2 men). The M.Gs of light horse all the camps should have given the raiders a good mark - the damage done was surprisingly small.	
			In the morning the Regiment was preparing to move back to BUSSY, but at 12 noon received orders to saddle up for a move forward, marched 4-	
MAMETZ	26		to MAMETZ at 4.30 p.m. & bivouacked there for the night.	
	27		Nothing came of the move on to attack the Brigade had been ordered, called up & to be marched back to DERNANCOURT bivouac at 9 a.m. & halted there for 4 hours.	

Army Form C. 2118.

p. 1119

WAR DIARY
of 36th Jacob's Horse
INTELLIGENCE SUMMARY
1916

(Erase heading not required.)

Instructions regarding War Diaries and Intelligence Summaries are contained in F. S. Regs., Part II. and the Staff Manual respectively. Title Pages will be prepared in manuscript.

Place	Date 1916	Hour	Summary of Events and Information	Remarks and references to Appendices
DERNANCOURT	Sept. 27th	2.45 pm.	Marched to BUSSY. Heavy rain en route. Bivouacked N. of village for the night. (Brigade Camp.)	AB
BUSSY.	28th	8.30 am	Marched to CROUY. Went into billets for the night. Horses in fields outside.	AB
CROUY	29th	8.30 am	Marched to PONT-REMY. Billets for the night. Rain on the march and all day. Weather - fine	AB
PONT-REMY	30th	7.15 am.	Marched to CRECY. Billets.	AB
CRECY.				

[signature]
Comdg. 36th Jacob's Horse

SERIAL NO. 112.

Confidential

War Diary

of

36th Jacob's Horse.

FROM 1st October 1916 TO 30th November 1916.
         31st October 1915.

Army Form C. 2118.

P. 119

WAR DIARY of 36th Jacob's Horse
INTELLIGENCE SUMMARY

1916.

(Erase heading not required.)

Instructions regarding War Diaries and Intelligence Summaries are contained in F.S. Regs., Part II. and the Staff Manual respectively. Title Pages will be prepared in manuscript.

Place	Date	Hour	Summary of Events and Information	Remarks and references to Appendices
CRECY	1916. Oct. 1 to Oct 31		Regiment in billets at CRECY, carrying out Regimental, Brigade & Divisional training.	nil.
	Oct. 28		A working party of 1 British Officer (Lieut Braithwaite) 2 Indian Officers + 30 other ranks proceeded, in part of a Divisional working party, for work in the XIII Corps area.	nil

W.H. Green Lt.Col.
Comdg 36th Jacob's Horse.

Army Form C. 2118.

p. 120.

WAR DIARY
of 28th Jacob's Horse
INTELLIGENCE SUMMARY
1916

(Erase heading not required.)

Instructions regarding War Diaries and Intelligence Summaries are contained in F.S. Regs., Part II. and the Staff Manual respectively. Title Pages will be prepared in manuscript.

Place	Date 1916	Hour	Summary of Events and Information	Remarks and references to Appendices
CRECY	Nov. 1		Billets at CRECY.	
QUESNOY LE MONTANT	" 2		Regiment marched (14 miles) to winter billets at QUESNOY-LE-MONTANT, LE MONTANT and CAHON — Regimental H.Q. at QUESNOY-LE-MONTANT.	
	" 11		The French working Party, under Lieut Braithwaite, that proceeded to the neighbourhood of HEBUTERNE on 28th October, rejoined the Regiment. Routine work.	
	" 12			
	" 15		CAPTAIN M.M. CARPENDALE proceeded to ENGLAND in charge of a detachment of Indian officers & men of IND: CAV: DIVN:	
	" 21		Regiment supplied "B" Coy: LUCKNOW PIONEER BATTN: proceed to 'SOMME' Battle front { Ha { CAPTAIN M.B. PARNELL - ADJT PIONEER BATTN: Battn { 9 I.O. Ranks.	
			CAPTAIN A.M. FORTEATH - O.C. COY: F.R. FARQUHAR - 2/I/ Command. LT. H.R. LANDALE } Itself Coy: Comdr: 2/LT. M.H. SMITH Indian officers - 5. Indian O. Ranks - 253.	

Army Form C. 2118.

WAR DIARY
of
INTELLIGENCE SUMMARY

1916 36th JACOBS HORSE

(Erase heading not required.)

Instructions regarding War Diaries and Intelligence Summaries are contained in F. S. Regs., Part II. and the Staff Manual respectively. Title Pages will be prepared in manuscript.

P.121

Place	Date	Hour	Summary of Events and Information	Remarks and references to Appendices
QUESNOY LE MONTANT	Nov. 27		A party of 28 I.O.R. arrived from ROUEN (Sikhs 19 - Banquet 9)	was
"	-25		A party of 28 I.O.R. proceeded to MARSEILLES in exchange for above detachment	was
"	-27		M.G. Squadron returned from participation in the SOMME BATTLE. They proceeded to the front line on 20.10.16.	was
	1.12.16			

J.M.Davidson Major
for O.C. 36th Jacob's Horse

SERIAL NO. 112.

Confidential

War Diary

of

36th Jacob's Horse C.I.J.

FROM 1st December 1916 TO 31st December 1916.

Army Form C. 2118.

WAR DIARY
of 36th Jacob's Horse
INTELLIGENCE SUMMARY
(Erase heading not required.)

1916

p. 122.

Place	Date	Hour	Summary of Events and Information	Remarks and references to Appendices
QUESNOY LE MONTANT.	1916 Dec 1.		Billets:- QUESNOY, LE MONTANT, & CAHON.	
	Dec. 6.		2nd Lieut T.F. JOHNSON, J.A.R. joined the Regiment from Base.	
"	" 9		Students rejoined from 4th Cavalry Division School, to which they went on Nov. 16:- Lieuts. Braithwaite & Ogley; Ressaldars Ibrahim Eng & Mahomed Nur Khan, Jemadars Alam Sher & Iltaf Husain.	
"			Jemadar Iltaf Husain proceeded to ROUEN as an instructor at the adv. Base Depôt, to relieve Jem: Nur Khan.	
"	" 13		Relieving Party for Pioneer Battalion left Regtl H.Q.:- 3 Br. Offrs (Capt. Blacker, Lt Braithwaite, 2nd Lt Johnson) 2 I. Os. 1 Br. O.R. 110 I. O. Rs.	
"	" 14		Moving in motor lorries to PONT-REMY; thence by train to EDGEHILL (ALBERT.) Relieved party from Pioneer Battn rejoined 4 Br. Offrs (Capt.ns Forsythe & Pennell, Lt Laudale, 2nd Lt Smith.) 2. I. Os. 116 I.O. Rs.	

SERIAL NO. 112.

Confidential
War Diary
of

36th Jacob's Horse C.A

FROM 1st December 1916 TO 31st December 1916.

Army Form C. 2118.

WAR DIARY
of 36th Jacob's Horse
INTELLIGENCE SUMMARY
(Erase heading not required.)

1916

p. 122.

Place	Date	Hour	Summary of Events and Information	Remarks and references to Appendices
QUESNOY LE MONTANT.	1916 Dec. Dec. 6.		Billets: QUESNOY, LE MONTANT, & CAHON. 2nd Lieut. T.F. JOHNSON, J.A.R. joined the Regiment from Base.	AF. AF.
"	" 9		Students rejoined from 4th Cavalry Divisional School, to which they went on Nov. 16:- Lieuts. Braithwaite & Ogley, Ressaldars Brahim Bux & Mohammed Nur Khan, Jemadars Alam Sher & Iltaf Hussain.	AF.
"	" 13		Jemadar Iltaf Hussain proceeded to ROVEN as an instructor at the adv. Base Depôt, to relieve Jem. Nur Khan. Relieving Party for Pioneer Battalion left Regtl H.Q.:- 3 Br. Offrs (Capt. Blacker, Lt. Braithwaite, 2nd Lt. Johnson) 2 I.Os. 1 Br. O.R. 110 I.O.Rs.	AF.
"	" 14		Moving in motor lorries to PONT-REMY; thence by train to EDGEHILL (ALBERT.) Relieving party from Pioneer Batt: rejoined 4 Br. Offr. (Capt. Farquhar & Pennell, Lt. Lawdale, 2nd Lt. Smith.) 2 I.Os. 116 I.O.Rs.	AF.

2449 Wt. W14957/M90 750,000 1/16 J.B.C. & A. Forms/C.2118/12.

Army Form C. 2118.

WAR DIARY
of 36th Jacob's Horse
1916.
INTELLIGENCE SUMMARY
(Erase heading not required.)

p. 123.

Place	Date 1916	Hour	Summary of Events and Information	Remarks and references to Appendices
QUESNOY LE MONTANT.	Dec. 17		2 British Officers (Lts Lansdale & Smith) and 4 Indian Officers went to 4th Cav. Bri. School (2nd Course)	sgd
	18		Capt: Totcath rejoined from Lucknow Review Batt: - Capt: Carpendale rejoined from duty in England, in connection with Indian Officers leave.	sgd
	19-31		Nil.	sgd

W.H.Vincent Lt Col.
Comm 36th Jacob's Horse.

2449 Wt. W14957/M90 750,000 1/16 J.B.C. & A. Forms/C.2118/12.

www.ingramcontent.com/pod-product-compliance
Lightning Source LLC
Chambersburg PA
CBHW081530160426
43191CB00011B/1727